"Cole Nowicki's *Right, Down +* speed time machine held togeth wallet chains. It immediately transports to an era of CD collections, ripped band tees, and sibling video game rivalry. Nowicki recounts the cultural alchemy that launched *Tony Hawk's Pro Skater* to global ubiquity and charts its influence right up to the present day. A wholesome joyride full of delightful trivia."
— Sarah Berman, author of *Don't Call It a Cult*

"As one of the people whose life changed forever the first time I picked up a PlayStation controller, *Right, Down + Circle* perfectly captures how it felt to witness a subculture becoming an inescapable phenomenon. Nowicki deftly follows the trails left by the urethane wheels of skateboarding and how it would change video games, music, and culture as we know it. Written with a familiar and vivid lived experience, *Right, Down + Circle* charts how *Tony Hawk's Pro Skater* changed those of us who felt like outsiders as we tried to find ourselves on the digital and concrete pavements of the streets that raised us."
— Niko Stratis, culture writer

the pop classics series

#1 *It Doesn't Suck.*
Showgirls

#2 *Raise Some Shell.*
Teenage Mutant Ninja Turtles

#3 *Wrapped in Plastic.*
Twin Peaks

#4 *Elvis Is King.*
Costello's My Aim Is True

#5 *National Treasure.*
Nicolas Cage

#6 *In My Humble Opinion.*
My So-Called Life

#7 *Gentlemen of the Shade.*
My Own Private Idaho

#8 *Ain't No Place for a Hero.*
Borderlands

#9 *Most Dramatic Ever.*
The Bachelor

#10 *Let's Go Exploring.*
Calvin and Hobbes

#11 *Extra Salty.*
Jennifer's Body

#12 *Right, Down + Circle.*
Tony Hawk's Pro Skater

right, down + circle.

tony hawk's pro skater

cole nowicki

ecwpress

Copyright © Cole Nowicki, 2023

Published by ECW Press
665 Gerrard St. East
Toronto, Ontario, Canada M4M 1Y2
416-694-3348 / info@ecwpress.com

Editor for the press: Jen Sookfong Lee
Copy editor: Jen Knoch
Cover and text design: David Gee

Library and Archives Canada Cataloguing
in Publication

Title: Right, down + circle : Tony Hawk's Pro
Skater / Cole Nowicki.

Other titles: Right, down plus circle | Tony
Hawk's Pro Skater

Names: Nowicki, Cole, author.

Identifiers: Canadiana (print)
20230237266 | Canadiana (ebook)
20230237304

ISBN 978-1-77041-716-8 (softcover)
ISBN 978-1-77852-198-0 (PDF)
ISBN 978-1-77852-199-7 (Kindle)
ISBN 978-1-77852-197-3 (ePub)

Subjects: LCSH: Tony Hawk's pro skater
(Game) | LCSH: Hawk, Tony. | LCSH:
Video games. | LCSH: Skateboarders. |
LCSH: Skateboarding.

Classification: LCC GV1469.35.T66 N69
2023 | DDC 794.8—dc23

Printing: Marquis   5 4 3 2 1
PRINTED AND BOUND IN CANADA

This book is funded in part by the Government of Canada. *Ce livre est financé en partie par
le gouvernement du Canada.* We also acknowledge the support of the Government of Ontario
through the Ontario Book Publishing Tax Credit, and through Ontario Creates.

For those who grow older all the time,
who inevitably look older all the time, but still,
underneath it all, feel younger in their minds.

Contents

Prologue: A Risky Game about a Lost Toy   1

Spinning into Focus   11

Those That Spun Before   18

Bruce Willis's Pro Skater   28

Real Skateboarders, Just Pixelated   38

Defining Sound   56

The Personal, the Playable   64

The World Drops In   73

Franchise and Fall from Grace   83

Tony's Magic Touch   95

Buttons Pushed   104

Sources   114

Acknowledgments   119

Prologue: A Risky Game about a Lost Toy

Since the beginning of time (for our purposes, 1971 or so[1]), a dynamic has existed among siblings playing video games. Whether they were in an arcade, had their noses pressed to an old cathode-ray tube TV screen, or found themselves huddled over the glowing rectangle of a smartphone, the older sibling has always, *always*, hogged that shit. Perhaps not all older siblings were guilty of this: The bogarting of quarters, that unbreakable grip on a greasy Super Nintendo controller, the claim that the *phone is theirs and they don't have to let you play, you idiot.* But my older brother, James, certainly was.

For hours I'd sit in the basement of our childhood home, forced to watch as he and his friend Nathan mashed

1 Syzygy Engineering debuts the first commercial video arcade game, *Computer Space*.

buttons on the PlayStation controller. *Tomb Raider*, *Gex*, *1080° Snowboarding* — all games I initially witnessed more than played. Only when the two went outside to smoke the cigarettes that my brother would steal from our mother would I get my opportunity.

As we moved into the late '90s, James and Nathan, now in high school and in search of an identity to call their own, found a new hobby, something to cling to while floating through the cruel, confusing morass of their teenage years: skateboarding. Almost immediately, the width of their pant legs ballooned, swallowing their skinny, pale legs. The summer afternoons that once took place in the basement were now spent rolling around the driveway, wallet chains glinting in the sun, narrated by a new language I had no grasp of: ollies, kickflips, backside tailslides. It was all Latin to me. To most younger siblings, your older sibling's interests are highly contagious. So, it wasn't long before I put down the PlayStation controller — which, in a sudden shift, I'd begun to have almost unfettered access to — and began to go outside to watch Nathan and my brother try to master the taxing physics behind the ollie.[2]

At first, I didn't get it. All they did was fall, pant legs parachuting but not lessening the impact of their pimpled teenage skin on the concrete. I tried riding their skateboards in a few wobbly attempts but was eventually told to *get your own, dumbass*. Soon, I was back inside, proceeding to get lost in a universe of different video games, from the childlike

---

2 The foundational skateboarding maneuver, like a bunny hop on a BMX. It's an integral building block used in almost all other street skateboarding tricks.

benevolence of *Croc* to the murderous vampire lore of *Blood Omen: Legacy of Kain*. It was bliss. However, just a short few weeks later, Nathan and my brother returned to the basement. Smelling now of cigarettes *and* weed, they promptly evicted me from the PlayStation and popped in a new game.

The startup screen commenced. Sony Computer Entertainment's logo flashed amid a growing, groaning hum that gave way to an orchestral clash of crystal chimes and the reveal of the PlayStation logo and licensing statement. Then the name of the video game publisher, Activision, exploded into relief from stone, quickly followed by a new slate bearing the name of the video game production company, Neversoft. The "o" of their name was an eyeball impaled on a spike, looking around frantically as a guitar riff wailed. A startling image for a nine-year-old to take in, no doubt. But there was no time to digest the gore because the intro for the game at hand had started, and another, even louder crash of guitars filled the speakers. Suddenly, a gravity-defying skateboarder appeared, somehow riding upside down in a large wooden loop that looked like the Hot Wheels track I had packed away in the closet. As I struggled to understand what was happening, a name assembled itself from a tangle of silver shards on the screen in front of me: *Tony Hawk's Pro Skater*.

The quick pivot in identity that James and Nathan took was fitting, in retrospect. They'd become skateboarders because they were already outsiders, teased and picked on by their peers for not fitting the mold of the typical rural Albertan child. We didn't have 4x4s, Ski-Doos, guns, or a penchant for the outdoors. With skateboarding being decidedly uncool at the time, and without any existing social capital to lose, all becoming a skater meant was they now belonged to a community that understood and accepted them when no one else did — classic subcultural allure. They bathed in the knowledge that the "normies" couldn't seem to grasp: skateboarding *was* cool. And now, whether others knew it or not, *they* were cool. It wasn't until I watched my brother and his friend play *Pro Skater* that I finally got a glimpse of what it was that enamored them so.

When the intro of *Tony Hawk's Pro Skater* roars to life, the Dead Kennedys' "Police Truck" drives the action. Its thudding guitar riff accompanies the introductions of the professional skateboarders featured in the game. Quick highlights of each skater's real-world feats help establish a certain feeling of legitimacy, that this is what skateboarding *actually* looks like. For nine-year-old me, seeing pro skater Jamie Thomas do a benibonga[3] down two flights of stairs was a revelation. So *this* was what my brother was trying to do? I couldn't describe what I saw on the screen or the pull it had. The cacophonous mix of sound and action, the acrobatics that were completely

---

3 The benibonga is a much-maligned skateboarding trick invented by Lester Kasai. To execute it, the skateboarder must move forward, gain airtime (off a ramp, staircase, etc.), take their back foot off the tail of the skateboard, and grab the tail with their back hand before landing back on with both feet — an aesthetically unappealing series of movements. The trick is often confused with the benihana, which is technically the same trick but is done going up a ramp backwards and coming down forwards. "The idea was to do a fakie thruster without planting your foot," Kasai told *Jenkem*. He'd also say that he named it after a favorite restaurant that he and Tony Hawk would frequent, Benihana.

foreign yet absolutely inviting, left me in awe. It was a whole new world crammed onto a CD-ROM.

A world that other kids, who lived in bigger cities dotted with a once-dominant fast-food chain, had gotten a sneak peek of months earlier.

In the fall of 1999, if you ordered a Stuffed Crust pizza from any of Pizza Hut's 7,200+ participating locations, you likely received a PlayStation demo disc that featured samples of games like *Crash Team Racing*, *Final Fantasy VIII*, *Coolboarders 4*, *Ape Escape*, and *Tony Hawk's Pro Skater*. After popping the disc into their consoles and subjecting themselves to a 30-second Pizza Hut commercial about big, foldable New York–style slices, millions of kids had their first introductions to skateboarding — all thanks to the cross-promotional marketing efforts of two corporate behemoths looking to secure the interest of the youth demographic and the wallets of their parents.

The two-minute *Pro Skater* demo featured the game's first level, the Warehouse. The dark, somewhat dilapidated industrial space allowed room for exploration and learning, which was necessary. "I'd wager my avatar spent more time on his back than he did on his board during that first demo session," Marty Silva would write in *IGN*. But for players like Silva, this wasn't just about learning how to play a game plucked from a pizza box; it gave them an education in skateboarding itself. "To be perfectly honest, I'm not sure I knew exactly what a grind was. But by the time the *Tony Hawk's Pro Skater* demo was done with me, I felt like I had just taken a crash course and passed with flying colors." The demo also featured "Superman" by Goldfinger as its soundtrack, a song that would later be seen as the game's de facto anthem.

The demo was a highly effective piece of marketing. "On that disc was a *Final Fantasy* game, which at the time would've been selling millions and millions of copies, and everybody is talking about the Tony Hawk game instead," Chris Rausch, a former senior designer at Neversoft recalled in the documentary *Pretending I'm a Superman: The Tony Hawk Video Game Story*. Redditor Dudergator felt its impact too. "It was the first level and the only track was 'Superman' that ended right around the part he says 'telling me I have to change, telling me to act my age' and I remember going out and buying the [cassette] at a second-hand store 'cause I wanted to hear how the song ended."

When my brother finally let me play the full release, I piloted a teetering, pixelated Andrew Reynolds — another real-life professional skateboarder, only digitized — and experienced everything Silva and Dudergator had in the demo. The rush, frustration, and illumination of what skateboarding was and could be, as told to me by what I saw onscreen. I spent every moment I could exploring the game's nine levels, collecting the letters that spelled out SKATE, smashing boxes, breaking mall directories (more challenges), and getting as high a score as I could by stringing together an impossible series of tricks through a combination of button-mashing and semi-realized hand-to-eye coordination. *This* was skateboarding. I got it. I loved it.

It was a strange time to make a skateboarding video game. Following the multiple booms and busts of skateboarding's popularity — spanning the 1960s until the neon spandex–clad resurgence in the late 1980s — skating was, by the mid- to late '90s, once again firmly in a rut. The occasional pop-cultural blip offered signs of relevance beyond the bubble of core skaters who'd stuck it out. Sonic Youth's music video for their 1992 release "100%" was directed by skateboarder and future filmmaker Spike Jonze and featured skateboarding from Jonze, Guy Mariano, and Jason Lee (later of *Chasing Amy*, *My Name Is Earl*, and *Alvin and the Chipmunks* fame). Larry Clark's 1995 drama, *Kids*, featured real skateboarders, including the late Harold Hunter, acting out a fictionalized version of their lives in New York City. The Extreme Games (later rebranded as the X Games) launched in '95 in hopes of corralling a growing demographic of youth that wasn't tuning in to *Sports Center*. Their first event included skateboarding and other pseudosports that they assumed the kids would be into, like bungee jumping and sky surfing. Activities that would eventually reach their popular zenith in the '90s and could, outside of their core practitioners, qualify as simply a fad.

But these were still just blips. It wasn't a sure bet that the public at large would care about skateboarding enough to buy a whole video game about it — especially if the corporate powers that be had up until recently viewed it on the same plane of relevancy as *bungee jumping*.

Suddenly our house was filled with skateboarding magazines. The pages of *Transworld* (the only skate magazine available in Lac La Biche, Alberta, population 2,700) were pasted all over my brother's bedroom wall — I'd later get to sift through whatever spreads were left for my own. VHS copies of Zero Skateboards' video *Misled Youth* and Shorty's Skateboards *Fulfill the Dream* were a constant double feature on the basement TV when *Pro Skater* wasn't in play.

Jamie Thomas and Chad Muska, both characters in the game, owned and were sponsored by Zero and Shorty's, respectively, which is how my brother discovered the brands. Each company featured in the game had struck deals to allow their logos and graphics to be used throughout. When you choose your digital skater onscreen, you're also able to pick their board graphic or earn new ones by completing challenges in the game. Zero's iconic skull logo — a nearly direct rip-off of the skull emblazoned on the t-shirt of the troubled kid Sid in the 1995 Pixar film, *Toy Story* — seemed as cool as cool could get. (Zero still sells the 3 Skull Blood graphic featured in the game over 20 years later.) It only added to the appeal that you could also buy those boards at your everyday skate shop — the epitome of effective and well-executed brand synergy.

The video game led my brother to seek out those magazines and videos, where we were introduced to the world of skateboarding beyond the game. It seemed there were brands and personalities that *Pro Skater* had neglected to tell us about, an ever-growing cast of characters buried in those glossy pages and on magnetic tape. My mindspace began to fill with names like Mike Carroll, Stevie Williams, Rick McCrank, and Mark Gonzales — icons and legends in the making. Absorbing skateboarding culture seemed integral to getting better at skateboarding itself, so I devoured it. Each time James would bring home new skate videos like Chocolate Skateboards' *The Chocolate Tour* or Foundation Skateboards' *Nervous Breakdown*, it was a celebration. And I poured over each *Transworld* with religious fervor. I had to see what new tricks had gone down every month and follow the drama of team changes and shit-talking that was almost a surety in each interview, reading them every night before bed and memorizing nearly every word down to the photo captions (these tended to be bad puns or short vignettes describing a skater's poor hygiene on tour). Never a kid drawn to traditional team sports that demanded a certain level of fanatic commitment, I found myself nurturing an unfamiliar, tumorous fandom. This amorphous thing called skateboarding that I couldn't quite define — part physical, part identity-building, part window to another universe — had taken over.

There's always been contention around what skateboarding "is." Fugazi's Ian Mackaye is oft-quoted for describing skateboarding as "not a hobby. And it is not a sport. Skateboarding is a way of learning how to redefine the world around you." This is true, to an extent. Because while skateboarding does challenge one's view of the possibilities in our physical world and turn common architecture into obstacles, it is also quite literally a sport. An Olympic one at that. Some call skateboarding an art. Others, like art historian, writer, and skateboarder Ted Barrow in *Jenkem*, argue that "skateboarders can do graphics, some can even make art, but skateboarding itself is not an art. I define art as a language that functions on a purely symbolic level. Art is not a tool, like the skateboard."

What is this thing then? The thing I've personally been doing and have been in love with for over two decades? Sport? Art? Tool? I can quantify the ways it's defined my life. Skateboarding has brought me untold amounts of joy, introduced me to countless friends and a supportive community, and exposed me to new worlds of music, art, and even literature. Skateboarding has inspired me to write, as you've probably gathered with this book in your hands. I've spilled thousands of words about this indefinable entity over the years, devotions for a spirit or a piece of wood with wheels, or both.

Even if we don't know how to categorize it, I do know what got me into it. Made at a time when skateboarding had little cultural foothold, *Tony Hawk's Pro Skater* took bits and pieces from skate culture, wrapped them in a video game, and sold them to the public at large. It was a risky move, attempting to capitalize on a thing that to this day is unsure of what it is, and whose practitioners would be the industry's harshest critics. Considering the millions of dollars the game would rake in, the countless hours that kids like me would spend in front of it, and the lifetime I'd subsequently spend with a skateboard under my feet, trying to be good at this thing while pushing it toward a new purpose and personal definition each day — I would say it was a risky move that undeniably paid off.

1

Spinning into Focus

"A lot of it's just on faith and confidence."

— Tony Hawk

The fifth edition of the X Games took place in San Francisco, California, from June 25 to July 3, 1999. The scattershot collection of "extreme sports" comprising the games reeked of ESPN executives (the X Games being an ESPN property) grasping desperately at what the key youth demographic of the '90s would hopefully be into: street luge, wakeboarding, sport climbing, bicycle stunt riding, aggressive inline skating, freestyle motocross, skysurfing, and skateboarding were all potential flypaper for the kids tuning out from the traditional ball and stick sports.

Thousands of spectators packed into Piers 30 and 32 to watch it all unfold. There were memorable moments, to be sure, like 15-year-old Travis Pastrana winning gold in freestyle motocross with a score of 99 out of a potential 100, and then promptly having his entire $10,000 prize purse revoked after he took his bike on a celebratory jump out of the course and into San Francisco Bay. ("A youthful indiscretion," *SFGATE* called it, somewhat sarcastically, at the time.) Or 18-year-old American Catholic priest Aaron Shamy taking gold with a new speed climbing record, only to later quit the sport to become a missionary. But there's only one feat that would create a superstar, become integral to the growth of a "sport," and make an unforgettable meme that doubled as a historical moment: 31-year-old Tony Hawk landing the first 900-degree spin on a skateboard.

On June 27, the "vert best trick"[4] competition was underway. The format was a simple jam session on a half-pipe, the skaters going up and down its transitions performing harder and harder maneuvers. Whoever did the best tricks would win, simple as that. It featured five of the top vert skateboarders at the time, including Colin McKay, Bucky Lasek, Bob Burnquist, Andy Macdonald, and Tony Hawk. Lasek would land a torqued frontside 540 while Burnquist struggled to eke out anything besides one of his patented one-footed backside smith grinds.[5]

---

4 Colloquially, "vert" is a style of skateboarding that takes place in your more traditional half-pipe or "vert ramp" settings.

5 A smith grind is where one grinds with the skateboard's back truck and dips its front truck below the height of the obstacle being skated. As you might expect, a one-footed backside smith grind is where the skateboarder lifts their front foot off of the board during the trick. A bit of a goofy-looking maneuver, but difficult nonetheless.

Macdonald would "produce several tricks with names longer than a long thing," the host of Channel 5's short-lived Saturday morning program *RAD* would declare when recapping the event. McKay, of Vancouver, BC, landed a series of hyper-technical moves that had commentators certain he'd take the gold, with McKay even throwing his board out into an already raucous crowd once the contest time had officially expired. Hawk had already landed a varial 720, which was a tough trick, but unlikely to guarantee a win. So, he started to try the 900. Hawk was familiar with what he needed to do — how to rotate, how much air he'd need to make each rotation. This was a maneuver he'd been attempting for years to no avail, only ever earning consistent beatings, once even cracking his ribs on an attempt. Essentially, he'd already done everything to do with the 900 — besides land it. With all of that sitting in the back of his mind, he began to spin.

The aim of the first few tries wasn't to land back on the board; it was to get the feel of it, to make sure he could get the full rotation. "Every time I spun it, it was feeling pretty consistent, that usually doesn't happen," Hawk would later recall. His first efforts at the 900 came in 1986, meaning there were countless attempts between those initial tests and Hawk standing on the deck of that vert ramp looking over the San Francisco pier in 1999 — a near generation of failure.

The relationships skateboarders have with their tricks are unusual and unpredictable. With some, the two can go steady for years, like the skaters who do a kickflip every session to make sure the flick of the toe stays sharp and consistent. With other maneuvers, however, things can be more tumultuous. Each moment you spend time together is a fight, a caustic back and forth. Frustration will inevitably mount, and the skater may question why in the hell they're even trying when neither of them seems to want it. As they collide with the ground again and again, they begin to realize that this whole ordeal is a tragicomedy of their own making with themselves at the butt of every joke — and then they land one and it all makes sense. That anguish and toil are suddenly worthwhile.

In the decade Hawk had been struggling with the 900 so much had changed within skateboarding — and his career. In the 1980s, Hawk progressed from earning 85 cent royalty checks to banking upwards of $100,000 per year. Then, as it was wont to occasionally do up to that point, skating's novel grip on the public slipped, its popularity declined, product sales dipped, and the bubble once again burst. And as a young Hawk entered the early '90s, he found his career on the slide. The 20-something pro was suddenly a "fading vert skater," and the paychecks from his sponsors started to get halved each month as the demand for skateboarding gear waned. Despite being the winningest skateboarder of his era (eventually claiming the title of world champion 12 years in a row) who would occasionally dip into pop culture with endorsement deals and small roles in '80s films like *Thrashin'* (as Josh Brolin's stunt double), *Police Academy 4: Citizens on Patrol* (as David Spade's stunt double), and *Gleaming the Cube*, Hawk still struggled. To make ends meet and provide for his young family, he began taking freelance video editing jobs for other skateboarding brands, and on occasion, video game companies.

Then, in 1992 as skateboarding's semi-regular death knell once again rang loud and clear (especially for vert skating), Hawk decided to start his own skateboard company, the aptly titled Birdhouse. This was an attempt at establishing a safety net, the laying out of building blocks for a career in business as it seemed like his athletic career was coming to a close — even as he tried his best to prolong it. In an effort to remain relevant, Hawk even left the vert ramp and took to skating the streets, where popular skateboarding's attention had shifted after half-pipes fell out of favor. In Birdhouse's debut video, *Feasters*, Hawk can be seen sliding ledges and jumping down stairs in billowing t-shirts that swallow his upper body and threaten to consume his gangly stems. His blond mop hangs in front of his face, jumping and falling as he frontside 360 ollies down three and four stairs.

Despite the sorry state of the skateboarding industry at the time (the cover of *Thrasher* magazine's October 1993 issue featured a tombstone reading "Skateboarding, 1943–1993"), Hawk and Birdhouse would push on, releasing two more videos (*Untitled* and *Ravers*) before a much-welcomed sign of corporate interest emerged: the 1995 Extreme Games. The contest's debut was an opportunity for Hawk to shine on a nationally broadcast stage — which he did, winning seven medals (four gold, two silver, one bronze) across multiple events in the years before the 1999 X Games. This success reignited Hawk's career and led to him signing with the prestigious William Morris Agency (now WME), who would go on to help him score lucrative endorsement deals.

The talent management agency was behind many of the branded stickers ringing Hawk's helmet as he stood on that vert ramp overlooking the San Francisco pier, including inter-loping non-skate companies like Hot Wheels and Club Med. Their logos blurred as Hawk spun. 180, 360, 720, 900 — bail. But he was getting close. By the seventh try, he was landing back on the board, but the official time limit for the best trick contest had elapsed. Colin McKay had tossed his board into the crowd in celebration of a victory that was surely his. Then a producer whispered in the MC's ear and Hawk was encour-aged to keep going.

"Tony Hawk. 900. This is it. Do it, do it, do it," the MC screamed into the mic, their voice growing hoarse from the goading. In the footage, the crowd erupts after each attempt, a stark contrast to the focus on Hawk's face. A stoicism that is only broken by a cry of frustration after he nearly rides away.

"Nine. Nine. 900!" Hawk spins. Two-and-a-half full rota-tions before collapsing at the bottom of the ramp. On the broadcast, every time Hawk found himself down there in a heap, he was backlit by the rotating digital ads on the crowd barriers. Skateboarding history, brought to you by Taco Bell, Starburst, the Marines, and Disney's *Tarzan*. Before his eleventh attempt, Andy Macdonald, Bucky Lasek, and the MC all place their hands on Hawk, as if performing some sort of transfer-ence of energy that X Games commentator Sal Masekela would later describe as them starting to "sprinkle the heebie-jeebies on him."

"Everyone picture it. Here we go!" the MC shouted. Then the crowd hushed as Hawk dropped in and went back and forth on the ramp, gaining speed, pushing himself higher into the air before reaching the lip of the ramp one more time. 180, 360, 720, 900 — make. Hawk finally rode away, one hand dragging behind him, his eyes wide as people rushed over the barriers to swarm him, lifting him onto their shoulders as if he'd just won the Larry O'Brien. "If it weren't for you people, I'd never have made that. Thank you. Thank you. This is the best day of my life, I swear to god," Hawk told the crowd as they continued to roar around him, his wife and child just feet away.

It would end up being the most consequential day of his professional life. Landing the 900 on national television broke Hawk out of the "action sports" bubble and placed him firmly into the mainstream consciousness. It was perfect, unplanned promotion for what was to come just over a month later: the release of *Tony Hawk's Pro Skater*.

2

Those That Spun Before

In the same way that skateboards themselves evolved — from pseudoscooters with clay roller skate wheels to the grip-taped popsicle stick–shaped urethane-enhanced setups of today — skateboarding video games have gone through their own evolution, from classic arcade games to console titles to mobile phone downloads you play with the tap and flick of your fingers. The initial entries to the genre appeared in the late '80s, as skateboarding still rode the spandex-clad wave of its penultimate boom period, buoyed by its brief forays into the Hollywood limelight with films like *Thrashin'* and *Back to the Future* that helped it maintain its grip on pop culture's imagination. Each addition to the nascent genre showed that there was at least some interest in skateboarding-themed video games, laying the slow, uncertain groundwork toward *Pro Skater*. Each title inching closer to something representing actual skate-boarding — with some zigs, zags, and bizarre detours along the way.

720° (ATARI, 1986)

In 720°[6] you pilot a neon-clad skateboarder around Skate City, a pixelated community full of ramps, surly skate shop owners, roller skating skeletons, and swarms of bees that — if your timer runs out while exploring the city and you have yet to choose an "event" — chase you throughout the streets to expedite your decision-making. The goal is to compete in a series of different events, including Downhill, Jump, Ramp, and Slalom. As the game's official materials describe it, "It's just you, your trusty skateboard, and a hundred bucks as you skate, jump, slide, spin and move through four levels of diffi-culty, picking up loose cash, earning money through events, and finally, earning a ticket to one of the big skate parks! If you're lucky, you'll get to buy some rad equipment to make you the coolest skateboarder alive."

It was a stilted and reductive interpretation of popular skateboard culture at the time, and it's a video game that needed to appeal to masses of children, so some grains of salt should be applied. However, the game's core of consumerism is still an accurate take on skateboarding, even now. That

---

6 Coincidentally, Tony Hawk was the first skateboarder to land a 720 spin on a skateboard in 1985.

nebulous state of "cool" is one most skateboarders in their youth try to attain via brand-name goods. My early childhood was marked by drawing the logos of skateboarding companies like Toy Machine, World Industries, and Zero onto my aquamarine social studies binder with a black Bic ballpoint, even if I didn't have the cash to buy their products.

So, the 720° declaration that purchasing "rad equipment" would "make you the coolest skateboarder alive" is not off-base with the cultural ethos that the industry relies upon to help sell its products. But it is decidedly uncool to say it out loud. Attaining and maintaining coolness is an unspoken central tenet of skateboarding. It's what most skateboarders strive for through the tricks they perform, the clothes they wear, and the attitudes they hold. That's why I, like so many others, would eventually trade in my baggy jeans for pants two sizes too small when the winds of skateboarding's fashion trends started to blow in the short-hemmed, skinny direction in the mid-2000s. It's this self-perceived cache of intracultural appeal that eventually caught the eye of the public at large, because "cool" has and will always be a resource that is in continuous demand, something that marketers know very well as they harvest that cool and sell it back to us; like OK Soda's attempt to reduce and package the growing disaffected nihilism of the early '90s grunge era as a soft drink. In the way most things that reach certain heights of popularity, skateboarding would eventually be twisted into easy-to-digest stereotypes by those outside of the industry.

720° would begin the trend of video games caricaturing skateboarding and skateboarders in the same ways that other pop culture media like movies and television did — as loud, brash, and distinctively anti-authority. It was this co-opting and flattening of the skateboarder's idea of cool that would get regurgitated back out in the form of the Daggers, a roving gang of denim-vest-wearing bad boys that terrorized the public in *Thrashin'*, or the inevitable coupling of Bart Simpson's irreverent delinquency with, of course, a skateboard.

SKATE OR DIE! (ELECTRONIC ARTS, 1987)

Those same flattened traits would carry over into *Skate or Die!*, a PC and console game from Electronic Arts (a company that would publish the genre-defining competitor to *Tony Hawk's Pro Skater*, *Skate*, decades later). Characters in *Skate or Die!*, like the aging blue-mohawked skate shop owner Rodney Recloose, his green-mohawked son Lester, and Aggro Eddie, are stereotypes of a hyper-masculine punk ethos that is now, at best, distantly charming, and at worst, woefully cringey.

The game consists of multiple events, like Downhill Jam, where you race down a pixelated city street, smash bottles, dodge open maintenance holes, hop onto cop cars, and punch your opponent for extra points. In the one-vs-one Pool Joust challenge, you roll back and forth across an empty swimming pool, attempting to either dodge strikes from Poseur Pete, Aggro Eddie, and Lester (each one represents a different difficulty level, Lester being the biggest and toughest of the bunch) or send them flying off of their boards with what appears to be a jumbo-sized Q-tip. The game was not well-received, earning only two out of five stars from Nintendo Life. A retro-review of *Skate or Die!* on GameFAQs from user horror_spooky was succinctly titled, "I pick 'die', thanks."

SKATE BOARDIN' (ABSOLUTE ENTERTAINMENT, 1987)

A pixellated avatar catching air in *Skate Boardin'* (Absolute Entertainment, 1987).

"Jump on that board and get psyched for a totally intense cruise!" shouts the tagline from *Skate Boardin'*, the compound-word-averse title for the Atari 2600. The way the game's official manual describes the premise is a fascinating prototype of how marketers would attempt to adopt skateboarding vernacular to help sell a product to a hard-to-define youth demographic:

> You know you're late for school, but what you don't know is that just overnight, an array of obstacles has been placed along the way. Radical man, this is a skate-boarder's dream come true! You have to get to school on time, but passing up the chance to ride ramps, or cruise tubes would make you look like a real nerd! You've got to conquer a total of thirty tubes and ramps in under five

minutes to be totally awesome. Not only that, after you find all the tubes and ramps you have to find the front steps of the school building. Check the ratings at the end of the instructions to find out how radical you are.

You don't want to look like a *real nerd*, now would you? Even if the in-game consumerism wasn't present, the desire to be cool — to not be a *nerd* — was still very much central to the messaging of the game.

CALIFORNIA GAMES (EPYX, 1987)

There were also strange permutations like *California Games*, a cross-platform multi-event game that featured "Californian" activities like surfing, BMX, roller skating, flying disc, footbag, and skateboarding half-pipe. The delightful absurdity of a Hacky Sack video game aside, this was one of the first games to acknowledge legitimate skateboarding brands, with Santa Cruz Skateboards being one of the teams a player could choose to represent.

A heated bout of footbag from *California Games* (Epyx, 1987).

ESPN EXTREME GAMES
(SONY INTERACTIVE ENTERTAINMENT, 1995)

In the early '90s, popular culture's interest in skateboarding would wane once more, and ramp skating, which dominated skateboarding for decades, faded into the background as the industry fell into another devastating decline. Most remaining "core" skateboarders took to the streets, where the freedom and creativity of skating in urban spaces had supplanted the stifling back and forth of the vert ramp. As the less TV-friendly and digestible-to-the-public "street skating" became the norm, the number of skateboarding video games dwindled as a result. There were guest appearances, however.

Following the debut of ESPN's Extreme Games in 1995, the worldwide leader in sports broadcasting decided they wanted to get in on the gaming market and partnered with Sony to release *ESPN Extreme Games* for the PlayStation that same year. While it did feature most of the sports included in the inaugural Extreme Games, strangely, instead of separating them into their respective categories, they all competed against each other — in a race. Mountain bikers, rollerbladers, street lugers, and skateboarders all clash for gold in a *Road Rash*–style melee. You don't do any tricks on your pixelated skateboard, but you are able to punch and kick your opponents into a speeding train somewhere in an arid Utah desert, if you so desire. This was emblematic of how the wider world saw skateboarding at the time, not so much a pastime but a gimmick merely worthy of pastiche.

Ronald McDonald, noted clown and burger chain mascot, would help the skateboard reach its apex as a prop by accidentally stepping on one in a late '90s television commercial, and getting uncontrollably whisked through the city streets, crashing through a department store, clothesline, and up the wall of an apartment building, before finally landing in a McDonald's restaurant. "Glad you could make it, Ronald," Birdie the Early Bird admonishes him flatly.

TOP SKATER (SEGA, 1997)

A couple of years following *ESPN Extreme Games*, skateboarding returned to the arcade with *Top Skater*. Here, the player spends a quarter to stand on a full-size skateboard-shaped controller, leaning to the sides to direct their onscreen skater down winding three-dimensional courses full of ramps, ledges, quarter-pipes, and whatever else Sega's developers deemed skateable. It's a fully realized arcade-ification of skateboarding. You speed through levels collecting *Sonic the Hedgehog*-like rings and time bonuses, stepping on the nose or tail of the controller[7] to execute different tricks that have only a loose connection to actual skateboarding, like the hyper kickflip, which doesn't resemble the simple horizontal flip of the kickflip and looks something more like a 360 triple kickflip in common skateboarding nomenclature (the board doing

---

7 The front of the skateboard is its "nose," the back, its "tail."

a full clockwise rotation while flipping horizontally three times over). It would be an aesthetically ghoulish maneuver to execute in real life, but it is perfect for the surreal nature of an arcade game. And this would be the first full three-dimensional skateboarding game, a style that *Pro Skater* and many others would go on to emulate.

Top Skater is also where we began to see a more advanced permeation of brands into video games. Banners for eS footwear, Etnies, Vans, Airwalk, and REEF are plastered along the perimeters of the courses, and the characters in the game are clad in their products, which are mainly shoes. Each shoe model featured is also noted, along with actual product photos, in the game's credits. The NASCAR-level of advertisements within the game is a jarring juxtaposition to its soundtrack, which is comprised of ten songs from the punk band Pennywise. The band screams about the societal pressure to conform as you grind past a giant Coca-Cola logo, Coke being the game's "presenting sponsor," its blinding red and white logo visible in nearly all sections of the game.

STREET SK8ER (ELECTRONIC ARTS, 1998)

Street Sk8ter is another three-dimensional time-based offering, this time for the PlayStation, and the console's first legitimate attempt at the genre. The player races through a track, attempting to score as many points as they can by doing tricks on a variety of obstacles. *You're ripping! Sick move! Crazy launch!*

An unknown announcer bellows as you button-mash your way through maneuvers. *Medic!* he cries as your character slides across the concrete on their face.

Street Sk8er is a charmingly ham-handed effort to distill the essence of skateboarding into a video game, perhaps even the best approximation up until this point. The game's soundtrack is pulled from a consistent catalog of '90s punk, and the tricks that your character can execute are, for the most part, correctly named and resemble what they look like when done in real life, unlike the loony arcade-ism of *Top Skater*. While it's an admirable attempt, it's still not great. *Next Generation* magazine was not as charitable at the time, saying, "Street Sk8ter [*sic*] is mildly diverting, but it just isn't polished enough to be a standout title. Skateboarding fans will just have to keep playing *720°* until a triple-A skating title hits the market."

Skateboarding fans wouldn't have to wait long.

3

Bruce Willis's Pro Skater

Tony Hawk loved video games. He was a self-described "arcade kid." It's not hard to imagine that what reeled him in is the same hook that has caught most players over the years: the ability to exist in a separate world for minutes, hours, or however long your cache of quarters can hold out. You can die and come back, lose and become the hero once more in short order. Video games can be brutal in their difficulty while simultaneously offering grace as they allow you to try and try again. Those quick releases of dopamine your brain gives you, especially while playing more fast-paced, action-oriented games, probably don't hurt either.

It's not unlike skateboarding, which can be unforgiving in its difficulty, but immense in emotional, physical, and even spiritual payoff. Once, as a ten-year-old, I spent hours attempting to learn heelflips in the driveway of my childhood home. Standing in place on my skateboard, I kept repeating the same simple motions: step on the board's tail with my back foot to make its front end pop up, then jump and slide my front foot up and off the front edge of the board. Theoretically, those movements done in concert will result in a heelflip. But they hadn't, even though I'd done everything I thought I'd needed to do, having decoded the step-by-step instructions to the trick by playing and rewinding pro skateboarder Steve Olson doing a switch heelflip in the Shorty's Skateboards video *Fulfill the Dream* countless times.

Still, I kept putting metaphorical quarters in the machine, even as frustration mounted and my focus began to slip. Then on one attempt, I jumped and kicked my lead leg straight forward, not in the up-and-out motion of Olson's that I'd studied so closely. As a result, the board shot up into the vertical position, my beloved toy now a skewer. First, I felt a white heat and then heard laughter as our neighbors across the street witnessed me thoroughly popsicle[8] myself on my skateboard. I ran inside, scared and shocked, to ensure I hadn't severed anything in that tenderest of regions. Not an hour after I'd confirmed all would be okay, I was back in the driveway, quarters in hand.

It could be described as urgent, that incessant need to get back up and try again. To regain composure, push through the adversity and embarrassment to keep progressing. To prove to yourself and your neighbors that they wouldn't be laughing

---

8 A cursed, self-explanatory visual.

long once you'd finally mastered your trick (even if they would bring up your popsicling multiple times in the coming years). It's a somewhat twisted measure of how bad you want a thing. There's no set limit to the suffering you can put yourself through, and there's no guarantee you'll succeed. What you're bleeding for is fractions of seconds and a feeling of satisfaction that, if you're lucky, sits with you for a few hours or days before you need to go back out and earn it again. But the most twisted part of it all is that it's *fun*.

In the early 1990s, pre–*Pro Skater*, a PC developer approached Tony Hawk about making a skateboarding video game with Hawk as its face. This game ran on a crude engine with clunky keyboard commands and was a generally unwieldy product. But there were issues beyond playability; the developer eventually encouraged Hawk to take their idea and pitch it to various publishing companies, but, "it just came up against a lot of hesitation, a lot of negativity. People just said, 'You know skateboarding is not popular; why would a skateboarding game be popular,'" Hawk recalled in *Pretending I'm a Superman: The Tony Hawk Video Game Story*.

The rejections were frequent and damning enough that the project was soon canceled; this was the first failed attempt at building a video game around the image of Tony Hawk. However, there was hope in this loss; the developer told Hawk that even though this project didn't stick, he was now a known entity in the video game industry. If the idea of a skateboarding game ever resurfaced, Hawk's brand recognition would make him a shoo-in as the person to front it.

As foretold, not long after the PC project tanked, Nintendo invited Hawk to their offices for a meeting — that ultimately went nowhere. But he got back up, regained composure, and eventually, Take-Two, the owner of Rockstar Games (publisher of the *Grand Theft Auto* and *Red Dead Redemption* series), would find their way to him. In 1998, they had started working on a skateboarding game of their own and felt Hawk would be the perfect name to attach to it.

He liked what they were doing. The developer (Z-Axis) was creating something close to a skateboarding simulator, a game that translated the bodily techniques and physics that skateboarders employ in real life to the buttons of a video game controller. This simulation could be as brutal and frustrating as the real thing, its learning curve tremendously steep. And in an added effort to make the game more realistic, if your character bailed, it could lead to broken boards or bones, which would force you to restart your runs.

While these were all novel concepts, Hawk was beginning to feel that Rockstar's game would be too challenging to master and would drive away potential players. Any game with his likeness attached had to be accessible and fun right off the jump. Because for Hawk, this was about more than just making a video game; it was the opportunity to introduce an entirely new generation to skateboarding.

Like the PC developer had predicted, Hawk was now a known and viable name in the gaming industry, which led to some competition for said name. While he was still in talks with Rockstar, Hawk received a call from Activision. The storied video game publisher had heard that he was working on a title, but they had one of their own that they'd like to talk to him about. It was being worked on by an upstart development company called Neversoft. Their small team had been given the opportunity to work on the untitled skateboarding project after winning substantial favor with Activision for saving a struggling game that had been spinning its wheels in development for three years.

That project was a third-person shooter called *Apocalypse*. Initially, it aimed to be a "'virtual buddy' game, emulating the buddy movies you'd see in the theater," said John Spinelli, the game's early art director, in an interview with *NEXT Generation*. Your buddy? That would be renowned scientist Trey Kincaid, played by action star du jour, Bruce Willis. Your goal? To stop a mad scientist, the Reverend, from bringing about the apocalypse (obviously) via the four horsemen that he has cooked up in his lab. Nu metal, trite religious references, and hokey sci-fi helped tie this powerfully '90s ensemble together.

However, the developers at the time were unable to get the "virtual buddy" AI system to function in a way that would allow you to team up with Bruce to shoot rocket propelled grenades at aliens without significant gameplay issues. Eventually, Neversoft was brought in and given six months to finish the job, a timeline leading to the most lucrative season of the year: Christmas. Their team quickly scrapped the buddy system, slapped Willis's likeness onto the main character's body, and edited the voiceovers the action star had recorded. It required a substantial paring down of lines since Willis's character was initially meant to be a mere sidekick, leaving their new hero with limited, stilted dialogue. Willis's character would infamously go on to shout inanities like "trick or treat," "strap one on, it's time to jam," and "yada yada yada" while in the midst of decimating alien hordes. Despite those hiccups, the team at Neversoft, in Herculean hunched-over-keyboards fashion, was able to crank the game out just in time for the holiday season of 1998.

Ultimately, *Apocalypse* became more of a punchline than a blockbuster, but it was still a serviceable game that helped recoup the money Activision had sunk into it over the years it sat mired in development limbo. This success led Activision to offer Neversoft the skateboarding project. Initially, there was some dissent among the team; many of them worried (and rightfully so at the time) that skateboarding just wasn't popular enough to carry the interest needed to make an impact in an already crowded video game market. But Scott Pease, a creative director at Activision who worked with Neversoft on the series, had grown up skateboarding. He'd been steeped in the skateboarding games of yore, like *720°*, *Skate or Die!*, and *California Games*, and was confident in the project immediately. Neversoft got to work.

First, they built a demo level, recycling much of the same code from *Apocalypse*. Enough so that the main character in the demo was still Willis, with a futuristic machine gun strapped to his back as he piloted a skateboard from rooftop to rooftop. It was a start, but the team still needed a hook, a name to attach to the game that would help it break through the noise and add a sense of legitimacy to its brand. So they got on the phone.

As the story goes, about a year before *Pro Skater* was eventually released, Tony Hawk entered an Activision boardroom in a t-shirt and ripped-up cargo pants; executives in suits flanked him on all sides. They showed him PowerPoints, revenue projections, and key market indicators until he began to slump in his chair. Mercifully, at the end of the meeting, a television was rolled into the room, the demo Neversoft had put together was turned on, and Hawk was handed a controller. He then directed a skateboarding Bruce Willis around a postapocalyptic wasteland. The controls were intuitive, the physics arcade-y but still realistic enough, and most importantly, the fun was immediate. "As soon as I played it and I felt some of the controls, I knew that was the game," Hawk would say in *Pretending I'm a Superman*. After eating shit on multiple attempts, he'd kept trying and finally landed it: a game fit for his name.

The news that Hawk was leaving their project to partner with Activision left Rockstar without a recognizable name to attach to their game. Eventually, they would go on to collaborate with one of skateboarding's most storied magazines, releasing *Thrasher Presents Skate and Destroy* on September 26, 1999. This was a game designed to speak to a core audience of skateboarders, and they'd clearly taken guidance from the higher-ups at *Thrasher* to make that a reality. Along with their simulator-style approach, which leaned into the authentic difficulty of skateboarding, the levels, characters, and game mode designs were peak '90s skate culture.

The six different playable characters (Axl, Cyrus, Jasmine, Kahli, Roach, and Scab) are clad in baggy pants, plaid, and tattoos. The game's levels are based on actual iconic skate spots, like the China Banks and Embarcadero in San Francisco, the Brooklyn Banks in New York City, and South Bank in London, England. You skate to an impressively curated soundtrack of golden-era rap and hip-hop, including songs from Sugarhill Gang, Grandmaster Flash, Eric B. & Rakim, Stetsasonic, A Tribe Called Quest, and Gang Starr.

In the game's Sponsorship mode, the end goal is, as you might expect, to get your character sponsored. It was a savvy move for *Skate and Destroy* to bake that journey into the game's narrative, with the player vying for sponsorship from brands like Converse, DC, Supreme, Alien Workshop, Antihero, and Independent on their way to becoming a pro skateboarder. For most young skateboarders, including myself, attaining some form of brand sponsorship was the dream. It's a strange, somewhat insidious way for capitalism to wriggle its way into the minds of youth, but boy did I ever try my hardest to earn the opportunity of becoming a living billboard. My friends and I took excursions to different cities, provinces, and even countries to film ourselves doing the best tricks we could in an effort to compile a "sponsor-me tape" to send to companies whose logos we pined to have pasted all over our bodies and whose paychecks we assumed would allow us to build a life around the only thing we could imagine ourselves doing.

To achieve that professional status in *Skate and Destroy*, you simply have to complete all the levels on *expert* difficulty. If you hadn't already broken your PlayStation controller in a whirling fit of frustration by that point, you could then attempt to climb the ultimate mountaintop in skateboarding: become *Thrasher*'s Skater of the Year — an actual award given out by *Thrasher* magazine that has only grown in relevance and competitiveness since *Skate and Destroy*'s release in 1999. How does the player earn the title of SOTY in the game? Oh, just by going back to "Destroy" all the levels in the game one more time, on *expert*, and then taking photos to grace five different covers of a pixelated *Thrasher* magazine in the process.

A punishing yet satisfying game, *Skate and Destroy* received generally positive reviews. Doug Perry at *IGN* summed up the gaming experience concisely: "You will get blisters, you will throw down the controller in frustration, and you will curse the game and its creators far more often than is morally right. But if you pull off the wall ride or a quadruple link, you'll be happy and relieved. And then you'll play some more."

Unfortunately for Rockstar's skate simulator project, it would never really take off. Instead, it would eventually attain a cult classic status as the years wore on, a game beloved by core skateboarders and masochists alike. Much like bailing a trick in *Skate and Destroy*, the game's lack of success would be a matter of timing, as all the oxygen had been sucked out of the market by a competitor that debuted just a few days later, one with a big, familiar name attached.

4

Real Skateboarders, Just Pixelated

Up until the late 1990s, photos and video were the only media of mythmaking in skateboarding, for better or worse. The skateboarding industry essentially created its own media apparatus to do this, with Fausto Vitello and Eric Swenson starting *Thrasher Magazine* to promote their company Independent Trucks. Subsequently, the lifeblood of every publication was the ad dollars brought in through skateboarding brands, which meant the magazines, in order to sell both copies and advertising, became quite adept at creating heroes out of the skateboarders who represented those brands. Mostly men and mostly white, these professional skaters existed on a separate plane. They even seemed to breathe different air. You, the young fan and skateboarder, were lucky to watch the legends grow in reputation in magazines and on your TV screen.

Occasionally, you'd get a glimpse of their personalities in an interview or some flash of B-roll, but never enough to create a complete human image. Instead, they were but a chalk outline that you could fill with whatever traits suited you and your friend group best. A brilliant, blank, and easily personalized marketing triumph.

Mike McGill, Steve Caballero, Lance Mountain, and Tony Hawk on the "Chin Ramp."

And in a culture as young as skateboarding, its initial architects are mostly still alive and able to be worshipped. Venerable skateboarding brand Powell Peralta released their seminal video *The Search for Animal Chin* in 1987. It immortalized skateboarders like Lance Mountain, Steve Caballero, Mike McGill, and Tony Hawk. A photo taken by J. Grant Brittain during filming of all four upside down on a vert ramp performing inverts[9] in sync, mere inches from one another, is one of skateboarding's most iconic images. It carries such historical weight that the four skaters recreated the photo — on a full recreation of the original "Animal Chin" vert ramp — 30 years later. These four men in bright neon, straining to stay upright, are a cultural touchstone. A large print of the original image hangs near the till of my local burrito joint in Vancouver, BC.

When a camera is pointed in the right direction, these brief moments — the seconds it takes to execute a trick or shoot off a witty one-liner — can make a skateboarder into something more. But, of course, a moment lacks nuance. Another iconic photo, taken by Craig R. Stecyk III in 1975 and featuring a young Jay Adams crouching as he speeds past a pylon in the middle of the street, is what most of his generation, and many that followed, remember about Adams. The grimace as his hand grazes the asphalt, style oozing from the very core of his being — he is skateboarding's original bad boy, a figure so iconic that he was played by Emile Hirsch in the 2005 film *Lords of Dogtown*. As Stacy Peralta (of Powell Peralta) would tell XGames.com following Adams's death in 2014, "[Adams] was the purest form of skateboarder that I've ever seen."

In August 1975, Adams was celebrated on the cover of *Thrasher*. He'd be on it once more in 1989. And yet, people don't often mention that he was charged with murder and convicted of felony assault following the beating death of a

9 A category of trick where the skateboarder is inverted, performing a handplant on the lip of a ramp.

gay man in 1982, a gruesome hate crime Adams himself would admit to initiating. The images, like the mythic ones of Jay Adams, lack necessary nuance. Even so, they still wield influence all these decades later.

Late in September 1999, there was an abrupt rewiring of how skateboarding's system of heroes operated, a new dimension added. You could now do more than just look at a professional skateboarder in a magazine or video, you could *be them*. *Tony Hawk's Pro Skater* was released for PlayStation, and, suddenly, the young fan and skateboarder could choose from an actual roster of professional skateboarders. From the titular Tony Hawk to Andrew Reynolds, Kareem Campbell, Bob Burnquist, Chad Muska, Rune Glifberg, Elissa Steamer, Bucky Lasek, Jamie Thomas, or Geoff Rowley. A scattershot collection of some of skateboarding's biggest names of the day.

Andrew Reynolds, who at the time was cementing himself as a generational star (one who'd later be known amongst his contemporaries as "The Boss"), had just released his now-classic video part in Birdhouse Skateboards' feature-length *The End*, frontside-kickflipping his place into history. Kareem Campbell's smooth brand of street skating had previously been showcased in World Industries' videos *New World Order*, *20 Shot Sequence*, and *Trilogy*, already placing him in the company of legends. Chad Muska was as close to a superstar as skateboarding had at that moment; the Shorty's Skateboards pro was as adept at marketing his personality as he was at skating.

Florida's Elissa Steamer, the beloved Toy Machine rider who'd made a name for herself in the company's videos *Welcome to Hell* and *Jump off a Building*, was already a pioneer of women's skateboarding by the time Neversoft came calling. Geoff Rowley came to the United States from Liverpool in 1994 with little money or regard for his own health and safety. Within a few weeks, he was on the cover of *Transworld Skateboarding*.

Then there were the game's vert skaters: Bob Burnquist, a Brazilian phenom; the hyper-technical Dane, Rune Glifberg; and Americans Bucky Lasek and Tony Hawk rounded out the roster's surprisingly robust vert contingent. This wildly talented bunch occupied a strange space within the profession, sometimes considered verifiable legends while, at other times, irrelevant relics once skateboarders took to the streets following the industry's last bust period in the '80s. "Vert button" became a common term for pressing fast forward whenever a vert skater's section started playing in a video. Despite a drop in status within skate culture, vert eventually found a new life on commercial network television following the debut of the X Games in 1995. Vert skaters began scooping up endorsement deals and raising their Q rating with the general public, even if that didn't often translate to popularity with core skateboarders. And now, here was an opportunity to become a character in a video game.

Until that point, starring in a video game was a step into the unknown. Who would be playing it? Would the game developers do your character justice? What if the game tanked? Was it even a cool thing to do? Maintaining one's "cool" and not "selling out" were many professional skateboarders' priorities at the time. Having one's likeness attached to a video game that ends up doing a disservice to the mercurial ethos of core skateboarding could be disastrous for one's reputation and career. Some skaters, like Jamie Thomas, were wary from the jump, as he explained in *Pretending I'm a Superman: The Tony Hawk Video Game Story*: "I had seen a lot of corporate entities come into skateboarding and . . . try and see what they could take from [it], and then they would just leave. [Leaving] whoever, whatever, high and dry. [Those corporate entities] didn't even care about the effect that they had on skateboarding. It was just, like, see how long they could make money off of it."

After decades of skateboarding being milked for profit whenever it resurfaced to the fore of popular culture, this was an understandable concern.

At the time, skateboarding was finding another foothold in the public consciousness thanks to nationally televised events like the X Games, which had Hawk as one of its poster boys. But the X Games were often seen by the core skate community as corporate schlock, so if you were concerned about remaining authentic, it was only natural to want to stay away from anything that could be considered inauthentic, an impulse that can be highly contagious. Thomas himself nearly declined the offer to appear in *Pro Skater*. "I knew that Tony was a little bit closer to the X Games and his persona was more wholesome and mainstream than mine was, so I was leery at the beginning and almost didn't want to do the game because I just felt like it was gonna be cheesy."

To help warm him up to the project, Thomas was given a list of his contemporaries who were to be featured in the game. Here is where the answer to the question of reputational risk versus financial and popular opportunity became glaringly obvious. Yes, he might fall victim to the cheese, but if he didn't participate, he would "be the one dude that isn't with his peers . . . [They] were going to be household names from this video game. And so, I did it."

Not everyone was as hesitant when they received the call, as Chad Muska recalled in *Pretending I'm a Superman*. "[Neversoft] were like, 'Do you want to be in a video game?' and I . . . couldn't even believe it was gonna be real, you know? . . . I remember thinking, like, that's just crazy. Skateboarding has got to that level that these major companies are going to invest [in a] skateboarding video game. I just thought it was the coolest thing ever."

Elissa Steamer seemed to land somewhere in the middle of those poles. In an interview with *GameSpot* before the release of *Pro Skater*, she was asked about her reaction to learning she'd be in the game. "I was excited when I heard . . . I was on tour, and my team manager, Billy, got a hold of me and told me about it." And when asked what her character would bring to the project, Steamer replied bluntly, "I am the only girl in the game."

Nearly 20 years later, Steamer recalled that moment again with a similar frankness for an interview with *SOLO*: "They called me and said, 'We want to give you that money to do this thing.' And I was like, 'Great!' And they gave me the money." That money, it would turn out, was initially quite substantial. In a 2014 interview with *Jenkem*, Andrew Reynolds claimed that each cast member received upwards of $190,000 for a single royalty payment. That was life-changing money for any pro skater at the time. (However, it wouldn't last, as Reynolds's anecdote continued, "But then some pro skater, I don't know who, went into the [Neversoft] offices and wanted to be in the game too. He told them he didn't care about the money, he would be in the game for free. So management was like, well . . . these guys will do it for free, let's just give them a flat rate for the next game. So that's what they started offering for the next games. It was a flat rate of 10k or something . . . But what are you gonna say, you know? I wasn't in any position or [didn't feel] like telling them that I didn't want the 10k.")

Beyond big-time money, being featured in *Pro Skater* offered its roster something only Hawk before them had known on that level: fame. A new level of notoriety, which had previously been confined to the bubble of skateboarding, began to seep out into the culture at large and change shape. "It was surprising to me, having built a career off of videos and doing tricks I wanted to do, and all of a sudden, my fans had doubled or tripled just from people who played the video game. I really didn't expect it when it happened. But everywhere I went . . . it was, 'Oh, I played you in the game!' Even still," Reynolds said in an interview with *ScreenRant*.

This transformation from a human skateboarder to a skateboarding video game character caused a confounding shift in public perception for some. "They don't know me for being an X Games gold medalist, or for being a professional skateboarder for 30-plus years, or being a rally car driver . . . they know me as a video game character. I'm still blown away by it," Bucky Lasek told *The Verge* in 2020, two decades after the game's initial release. That's the disquieting power of a pop culture phenomenon; it takes a moment in time, swallows the history that came before and after it, and flattens everything that remains.

While this separation from his achievements seems to be more of a curiosity for Lasek, with Steamer, there was frustration at being recognized as a video game character and not the person whose accomplishments had earned them the opportunity to be featured in a game. "I did the [game] and . . . people that were skating all over the place would recognize me. It would sometimes bum me out though. The mainstream only noticed you because you're in a video game and didn't recognize all the shit I had to learn to get into the video game. Like, I actually ride a skateboard. I'm not that digital being." That stilted form of fame aside, Steamer could still enjoy the other reality of being in a blockbuster game. "How did it change my life? It got me paid," she told *SOLO*. "I was able to buy a house and a car. I remember talking to [legendary professional skateboarder and owner of Toy Machine Skateboards] Ed Templeton about money when I was younger and he was like, 'You're fortunate if you get to buy a Honda Civic[10] off of skateboarding.' I'll always remember that."

Fame is a strange, nuanced thing. There is a decidedly dehumanizing aspect to it, the part that leads generations of kids and adults to shout "Do a 900" at Tony Hawk as if a life-changing moment can be replicated on command for the rest of his waking life. And modern celebrity generally creates depthless idols, but sometimes even a flat image can offer inspiration. For Chad Muska, decades after the game's release, "people [still] come up to me [and say] *Tony Hawk's Pro Skater*. I picked you! If it wasn't for you, I wouldn't have started skateboarding." Influence is another power bestowed on those who are a part of a pop culture phenomenon, for better or worse. That sway can be as transient as a one-hit wonder's or as sustaining as it has been for the cast of *Pro Skater*. Each member of the original roster is still relevant in the world of skateboarding, a decidedly young person's pursuit, even as they press on into their late 40s and early 50s.

"This game culturally developed a generation," Muska opined in a promo video for the remastered version of *Pro Skater 1+2* in 2020. That's quite a claim, but it's true in many ways, even for me. These skateboarders, these *digital beings*, were

---

10 The Honda Civic was the unofficial vehicle of the professional skateboarding class during this era due to its economy and gas mileage. Second, third, or fourth-hand Civics were preferred.

more influential to me than any movie star or musician that found their way onto the latest *Big Shiny Tunes* compilation[11] — especially when it came to fashion. I would adopt the tight jeans, hoodie-up look of Jamie Thomas for nearly all my pre-teen and teen years, going so far as to steal my mother's skinny jeans.[12] Thomas's Zero Skateboards and subsequent brands Mystery Skateboards and Fallen Footwear would dominate the industry for most of the '00s.

But it was Muska who would arguably become one of skateboarding's most recognizable silhouettes. His trademark basketball jersey and baggy capri-style swishy pants were an aesthetic template for an untold number of suburban white kids who were into skateboarding and hip-hop. And while this was true before *Pro Skater*, that influence only multiplied once his likeness appeared in playable form in the homes of millions. One of Muska's "signature moves" in the game involves his character performing a grind with a boombox slung over his shoulder — an homage to real-life Muska crooked grinding a rail at a skatepark demo in White Rock, BC, his trusty, soon-to-be iconic, boombox cradled in the nook of his arm. A deftly added detail by the game's developers that gave Muska's character real *character*.

In the years and *Pro Skater* sequels that followed, Muska's celebrity would extend further out of skateboarding's bubble than most. He'd eventually become something of a Hollywood

---

11 Much Music's once-annual album compiling the biggest hits in Canada. Every millennial Canadian owned at least two *Big Shiny Tunes* CDs.

12 Sorry, Mom.

socialite, covering the majority of the bases within that world — partying with Paris Hilton, becoming an artist, having a video of his drunken arrest filmed and published by *TMZ*. Andrew Reynolds would leave Hawk's Birdhouse Skateboards to start his own brand, Baker Skateboards, his persona of hard-partying and hard-charging skateboarding making him a superstar in his own right, one worthy of the title "The Boss." Kareem Campbell's brands CityStars Skateboards and Axion Footwear would help launch the next generation of skateboarding's big names before ultimately folding — the skateboarding industry can be an unforgiving one. After fading in and out of skateboarding's limelight over the next couple of decades, Campbell's induction into the skateboarding Hall of Fame in 2021 would give his career a jumpstart, leading him to revive his brands, and like most people in the 2020s, start a podcast.

Elissa Steamer would reach the status of icon in short order. Already a pioneer as a queer female professional skateboarder, she became the first woman with a pro model shoe (with Etnies), started her own apparel company, Gnarhunters, and eventually found a comfortable home with sponsors like Reynolds's Baker Skateboards and Nike SB. Skateboarding's premiere scouser, Geoff Rowley, would push his fearless, progressive brand of street skateboarding into the realm of legends. In 2000, he'd be crowned *Thrasher*'s Skater of the Year — a title he'd share with fellow *Pro Skater* castmates Hawk, Burnquist, and Reynolds.

The game's vert specialists, a group that still hasn't quite regained their former glory, would fare quite well. Bob Burnquist would take skateboarding to previously unknown heights, doing literal death–defying stunts on his personal MegaRamp — essentially a chasmic snowboard jump, but for skateboards — that are still unparalleled to this day. He even took his skateboard off a ramp, onto a rail, and into the Grand Canyon, because, why not? Bucky Lasek would become somewhat of a NASCAR-like entity within the realm of competitive skateboarding, adding sponsors like Subaru and Campbell's to the many logos already stickered across his board. Now, even in his late 40s, Lasek is still skating at a level that's hard to comprehend.

After living in the United States for nearly two decades, Rune Glifberg would return to his native Denmark in the early 2010s, eventually starting a skatepark design firm, Glifberg+Lykke, with his partner Ebbe Lykke. They've since built skateparks all across Europe. Glifberg has remained an active professional skateboarder, too, even competing under the Danish flag at the Tokyo 2020 Olympics. The 46-year-old would place 19th overall at the men's park event.

DIGITAL CHARACTERS, REAL WORLD EFFECT

And then there's Tony Hawk, who is currently everywhere, all the time. From appearing in Subway commercials to skating in backyard pools, the man remains ever-present. Skateboarding's fatherly ambassador. A shepherd who brought these nine other skateboarders into the fold, giving their careers new life with immortal digital avatars.

Hawk says he chose this group of skateboarders because in the late '90s, they were at the top of their games, finding and pushing beyond the limits of what was thought possible in their respective styles of skating. *The best of the best.* Another way to accurately describe the game's roster would be mostly men and mostly white. "Looking back, obviously, it was super skewed. There's only one girl. But at the same time, that was the state of skateboarding — the ratio of male to female was so offset. Elissa was truly the best choice in terms of the best street skater. Even with Kareem representing African Americans . . . That ratio is way more equal in skating now," Hawk told *The Ringer* two decades after the game's release.

For most of its previous existence, skateboards had been predominantly ridden by young white men. Toys used by blond-haired, blue-eyed surfers to cruise down suburban sidewalks when the waves were out. Does that mean there weren't other prominent women and people of color in skateboarding at the time who would've been a fit for the game? No. There most certainly were. If we wanted to attempt a rosy view of this, comparatively, it was impressive for a video game released in the '90s to have its character roster be only 80% white and 90% male. But then you'd have to acknowledge that your rose-colored glasses are smudged by the reality of the situation at the time.

Diversity in "human" video game characters has always been historically lacking, and is still, even today. DiamondLobby, a website that covers video games, looked at 100 titles released between 2017 and 2021, and found that 79.2% of the main characters were men and 54.2% of the main characters were white. Just 8.3% of the main characters in the games they studied were racialized women. How the few women characters in these digital worlds are portrayed is another thing. A bluntly titled study out of Oxford University in 2016, "Sexy, Strong, and Secondary: A Content Analysis of Female Characters in Video Games across 31 Years," analyzed 547 games released between 1984 and 2014 and found the overt sexualization of female characters reached its cringiest heights from 1990 to 2005. If you've ever played a video game, that's likely an unsurprising statistic.

There is actually more than one woman in *Pro Skater*. There's a secret, unlockable character named "Private Carrera." Dressed — a generous phrasing — in short shorts and a revealing tank top, Private Carrera is technically the best skater in the game. Her character stats (ollie, speed, air, and balance) are all listed at 100%, far surpassing everyone else. Her other stats? Well, the game lists her as from Fort Worth, she's regular footed, stands at 5'8", has been pro for one year, and her age is . . . "barely legal." This biographical tidbit would eventually be changed to "41" in the game's port for the more family-conscious console in the Nintendo 64. In addition, for many gamers who also happened to watch porn in the '90s, Private Carrera looked awfully familiar.

Neversoft developers, and even Hawk himself, would later have to go on record to quash the rumor that Private Carrera was based on adult film star Asia Carrera. However, by then, rumors about her inclusion in the game had reached the actual Carrera, who at the time contacted Neversoft. They denied the character was based on her likeness but would eventually extend a friendly invite and have her visit their offices as a guest.

Then there were the other non-playable women in the game. Also secrets, they were eventually found by intrepid (and likely confused) gamers. On the N64 version of the game, entering different codes into the game's pause menu would reveal the portraits of several unnamed women — a strange, somewhat spooky discovery, ripe for conspiratorial thinking. Many internet users assumed it was a bizarre tongue-in-cheek tribute to Hawk's girlfriends. (Hawk was married at the time of the game's release.) Eventually, Ralph D'Amato, a producer on the game, would confirm that the images weren't placed there by Neversoft but instead were Easter eggs left by developers from Edge of Reality, the company that worked on the *Pro Skater* port for Nintendo. The women in the images were, according to D'Amato, the significant others of some members of Edge of Reality's executive team. These strange Easter eggs were meant to be (strange) tokens of affection.

While the representation in *Pro Skater* was both lacking and at times bizarre, having characters like Steamer and Campbell in the game still made an impact. For players around the world to see a woman and a Black man skateboarding, to be able to play as them in a world dominated by gangly young white dudes, was eye-opening. "Seeing Elissa Steamer in there was like, 'Oh, you don't have to be just a guy to become a pro skater,'" Leo Baker, a trans and nonbinary professional skateboarder, told *Hypebeast* about his first exposure to the game.

"It really never hit me until it was acknowledged by some of the fans," Kareem Campbell told the *Dallas Observer* about the effect his character had on gamers and skaters of color. "It was crazy. Basically, if people identified as a minority, then in the game, they aimed toward me. Regardless of that, I definitely didn't look the way people thought a skater should look." Tony Hawk has echoed that, sharing with *The Ringer* that he's often approached by skaters of color who tell him that playing as Campbell inspired them to skate. Even Grammy-winning producer and recording artist Pharrell Williams. "He was telling me about growing up in Virginia, being a skater, and how it was just not cool in his region and his crew. He said after the video game came out, it was just normalized," Hawk recounted.

That's what representation can do at its best — inspire and empower. And on the most shallow, capitalistic level, if you're a multi-million-or-billion-dollar video game company, appealing to as wide a demographic fanbase as possible should already be the goal. The Entertainment Software Association's *2021 Essential Facts about the Video Game Industry* report found that 45% of American gamers identify as women, while 26% identify as non-white. Think of all the money just sitting there, Mr. CFO.

While there aren't reliable statistical breakdowns for skateboarding's demographic shifts, we can simply look around us: from the slow but steady growth and acceptance of women and queer folk in mainstream skateboarding media; community organizations like Takeover Skateboarding and Late Bloomers Skate Club in Vancouver, BC — whose goals are to help diversify their local scenes by providing safe and inclusive spaces for women, BIPOC, and LGBTQ2S people to skate; to the purely anecdotal, like how in the last three to four years, there's been a legitimate and noticeable growth in the number of women, queer folk, and skaters of color that I personally see when I go out skateboarding.

It's taken skateboarding a long time to reach this place, and there's still a long way to go before we see truly equitable growth and representation in the skateboarding media and industry, but small steps have been taken. And each one helped lay out a path for big names like Leo Baker and an untold number of people who have found in skateboarding a community, camaraderie, and just plain fun. So, while Steamer's and Campbell's inclusion in *Pro Skater* was not the biggest leap at the time, its impact has been felt across generations.

5

Defining Sound

You're walking through the grocery store's glowing aisles, plucking whatever the list in your Notes app dictates from the shelf and plopping it into your basket. The strategically tuned easy listening radio station seeps through the speakers above, broadcasting Céline Dion's "My Heart Will Go On." You wince slightly from the recognition as your mind cuts to Leonardo DiCaprio and Kate Winslet standing on the bow of James Cameron's *Titanic*. *I trust you.* As you remember the film's two VHS special edition boxed set that you begged your parents for as a child, you shudder.

A well-executed soundtrack can pull you into memories and even place you in a specific locus of a multi-billion-dollar entertainment property. Maybe Aerosmith's "I Don't Wanna Miss a Thing" summons Bruce Willis's oil-driller-cum-astronaut

Harry (spoiler) detonating himself and an asteroid to save all of humanity. The Soggy Bottom Boys' rendition of "Man of Constant Sorrow" might flash George Clooney's Dapper Dan–soaked scalp in front of your eyes. Any Smash Mouth song will likely drop you straight into the very muck of Shrek's swamp that he so desperately wants everyone else to get out of. Association exists outside of cinema too.

Bum-bum-bum bumbumbumbum bum^bum bum^bum bum^bum bum^bum ^bum bum^bum bum

If you've just read that aloud to yourself and you've been a person on this earth existing near popular culture over the last four decades, you probably recognized yourself *bum-bum*-ing the iconic refrain of the "Overworld" theme from the soundtrack to *Super Mario Bros*. This electronic pinging of a nearly 40-year-old video game holds as much cultural relevance as any pop song. It's also just as potent as a memory trigger, maybe transporting you to the basement of your childhood home, crowded around the television with your friends and family. You might feel your palms slick with sweat as your body remembers the hours spent gripping the controller in tense, full-body concentration. The knuckles of your thumbs aching as you unrelentingly mash the greasy buttons, Goombas flattening beneath the soles of Mario's feet.

Link's 8-bit heroics in the original *The Legend of Zelda* for NES are set to a now-iconic soundtrack from composer Koji Kondo. "How can a simple tune like this sound so freakin' EPIC?" one YouTube user commented under a rip of Kondo's "Overworld" theme for the game. "Legit one of the best tunes in the world. Still keeps that *adventure* feeling," another says. One commenter shared a more profound association: "This makes me cry. I'm seven years old again, and my mom is still alive, wanting to play gyromite." Whether a trolling remark or not — it is the internet, after all — the power even simple musical compositions can wield is immense.

It took years for video game soundtracks to reach even the basic level of arrangements that Mario and Link were hopping and slashing to. Initially, it was quick, primitive melodies made of short bursts of beeps and bloops. The first came in an arcade game called *Gun Fight* (Taito, 1975). In the *Pong*-like game, you and an opposing cowboy stand on either side of the screen trying to avoid the little balls hurtling out of your opponent's pistol. The action is set to a tinny, strangely charming rendition of the first few seconds of Chopin's "Funeral March."

Then gaming systems, including their sound hardware, started to advance, giving developers more freedom and creativity when composing soundtracks. In a span of just over ten years, the processing power of these systems' CPUs jumped from 8-bit to 64-bit. The original NES's five-channel sound chip would be eclipsed by the eventual debut of the PlayStation's CD-quality 24-channel version.[13] This advancement would allow for a move away from simple beeps and bloops and into the use of prerecorded music. Real guitars, percussion, vocals — the future was at hand *and* ear.

---

13 Each channel can play one audio signal at a time, e.g., one for melody, one for bass, one for percussion.

"Man, I don't know if there was songs in video games before *Pro Skater*," Larry "Ler" LaLonde, guitarist for the band Primus, incorrectly posits in the documentary *Pretending I'm a Superman: The Tony Hawk Video Game Story*. His band's song "Jerry Was a Race Car Driver" is featured in *Pro Skater*, but *Pro Skater* was not the first video game to feature prerecorded music from "legitimate" acts. It wasn't even the first skateboarding videogame to do so. The popular arcade game *Top Skater* used the punk band Pennywise for the game's entire soundtrack. *Street Sk8er* featured music from some of the most popular names in '90s punk, including Less Than Jake, I Against I, H2O, and Gas Huffer. And let's not forget *Thrasher Presents: Skate and Destroy*, which was released just days before *Pro Skater* and boasted a deep soundtrack of iconic rap and hip-hop.

To be fair to Ler, using CD-quality music in video games was still a new thing in the late '90s. He even recalls not fully understanding Neversoft's offer to feature their song at the time, as he'd never heard *music* music in a video game before. That's likely part of the reason *Pro Skater* is often attributed as being one of the first games, if not the very first, with a full soundtrack comprised of licensed music; it became iconic enough that it swallowed the short history preceding it. And for that generation of gamers weaned on *Pro Skater*, hearing the crash of cymbals and brass that leads into Goldfinger's "Superman" might just trigger a Pavlovian response, their right thumbs instinctively pressing at the air where the PlayStation controller's triangle button would be, preparing to grind.

"I asked my dad if he remembers this song. He smiled and said out loud 'that's the skateboard song!'" One YouTube user commented under an unofficial upload of "Superman" that has garnered nearly 14 million views. The song became so popular via the game that it changed the course of the band's trajectory. John Feldmann, Goldfinger's vocalist, would tell *Loudwire*, "I really didn't know how much Tony Hawk helped our band with that song until we were on tour in England. We were touring with Bloodhound Gang and supporting them as they had this huge hit at the time in Germany, so we played with them in England and all of a sudden when we played 'Superman,' everyone went ballistic. It was the biggest circle pit of the entire night. There was no moment in Bloodhound Gang's set or our set that surpassed what happened with that song. I was like, 'What the fuck is happening with this song?' But I put two and two together and realized that *Pro Skater* had globally just become this huge hit of a video game."

The soundtrack was a total of ten songs from the bands Goldfinger, Primus, Dead Kennedys, The Ernies, Even Rude, Speedealer, Suicidal Tendencies, The Suicide Machines, Unsane, and The Vandals. Hawk himself had a lot of input when it came to what music went into the first few games in the series. He told *Kerrang!*, "The soundtracks are very much in line with my music tastes and my history of growing up skating. Punk music was really closely associated with skating at the time and a lot of the songs on the soundtracks were songs that I heard growing up at skate parks."

Each track in the game would end up being a shortened, edited loop of its original form, as the game's two-minute timed run format and the game disc's limited memory didn't allow for the full songs to be played. For those two minutes of gameplay, the player is fed pulsing choruses, strictly peak tempos, and refrains that would be drilled and implanted into the user's brain with enough repetition. Two decades later, those lyrics still swim around in my own head, waiting to be pulled to the surface at the first whiff of a riff.

After noticing Primus's fanbase beginning to swell with gamers who discovered them thanks to *Pro Skater*, LaLonde joked that he worried fans would get sick of their music. "I thought it would be like, 'Dude, I can't listen to that song again, I've heard that loop a million times in my head playing the game. I love your band, but I can't hear that song again.'" That didn't turn out to be the case. People couldn't stop listening to it.

It didn't cost Neversoft much of their allotted budget for such an influential aspect of the game either. Brian Bright, an associate producer at Activision at the time who dealt with in-house audio, said to *Loudwire* that the entire soundtrack cost the company roughly $30,000. "Today you can pay that much for a single song!" A sound investment. One that would eventually develop a cult following, so much so that it inspired a cover band that strictly plays songs from the *Pro Skater* franchise soundtracks. Birdman or The Unexpected Virtue of a Tony Hawk Pro Skater Cover Band is a Sydney, Australia–based group that began playing shows together on a lark in 2018. Sim Bartholomew (the band's bassist) sent his friend Josh Newman (the band's eventual guitarist) the band's name, a riff on the Oscar-winning 2014 film *Birdman or (The Unexpected Virtue of Ignorance)*, as a joke, and the ensemble snowballed into reality.

Birdman played a handful of small shows before booking a headlining charity event in their hometown. In the lead-up to the show, they tagged Hawk in their promotional social media posts, eventually catching the eponymous Birdman's attention. "YOU GUYS!! TONY HAWK LIKED THIS!!!" They screamed in all-caps in the comments. That simple tap of the heart was victory enough for the band, but Hawk had other plans. He eventually sent Birdman a direct message on Twitter, asking what their setlist looked like and if they'd like to come out to California to play a charity event of his own for the Tony Hawk Foundation. (Now known as The Skatepark Project, Hawk's non-profit organization provides grants to low-income communities to build skateparks as well as offers guidance to city officials throughout the process.) That show coincided with *Pro Skater*'s 20th anniversary, and Birdman would have the opportunity to open for the legendary punk band Bad Religion.

(Bad Religion is featured on the *Tony Hawk's Pro Skater 2* soundtrack. Despite the impact of the original *Pro Skater* soundtrack, Hawk himself would say that his favorite game of the entire franchise is *Pro Skater 2*, specifically because he thinks the music in it is better. That soundtrack includes songs from Bad Religion, Rage Against the Machine, Anthrax/ Public Enemy, Papa Roach, Naughty by Nature, Powerman 5000, Swingin' Utters, The High & Mighty, Dub Pistols,

Consumed, Styles of Beyond, Millencolin, Alley Life featuring Black Planet, Lagwagon, and Fu Manchu.)

It all seemed too good to be true for the band, but Hawk would keep his promise, flying the entire group from Sydney to San Diego to play the show. In the days leading up to the event, the Birdman would spend a fair amount of time with the band, giving them a tour of his offices and vert ramp, stopping by their rehearsal, and even jumping on the mic to practice himself. Then, during the show, Hawk would join the band onstage, his signature Southern Californian drawl belting out The Adolescents' song "Amoeba." It was the end of a surreal whirlwind for the Aussies, all of it brought about by the soundtrack of a 20-year-old video game.

And as tongue-in-cheek as the musical project may be, Bartholomew holds a genuine reverence for *Pro Skater*, telling *Forte*, "The beauty of the game was that, for me, I had a massive injury as a kid. For a long time, I couldn't walk properly, I couldn't jump or ride a bike. So the game was a great outlet for me to be able to skate. It was so freeing at the time because I could do all the tricks and fly, I could skate in the most passive way possible but it meant so much."

That's a feeling millions of others would relate to. Whether spurred by the soundtrack into fits of nostalgia or buoyed by the freedom to fly their skateboards around a digital world that might be more hospitable than their own, *Pro Skater* was able to forge an emotional connection with its audience, doing the special thing that video games can sometimes do: become a refuge.

6

The Personal, the Playable

The space between knowing and not knowing is a labyrinth. Some labyrinths are simple and can be navigated without too much effort or danger; others are winding and full of dead ends and minotaurs of varying size and ferocity. These mazes materialize when you discover a thing you want to know more about. Getting to the core of that curiosity — or solving the labyrinth — requires a process called *learning*.

Maybe you want to make a spicy chicken and couscous dish for dinner. That meal is at the labyrinth's center. You must find your way to it. You Google a recipe, go to the grocery store, trudge home, prep the marinade, and start the vegetable broth on medium-high, taking each turn in the labyrinth with varying levels of confidence until the meat in the pan is no longer pink and squishy, the couscous is fluffed, and you're scrambling for a garnish. But, even if you do make your way to the labyrinth's center, that doesn't always mean you'll get out unscathed. The minotaur can still take a pound of flesh. Your chicken breast could end up dry and flavorless. But it's a start. Repetition is key. Practice until you remember which of the labyrinth's hallways have the loose cobblestones that keep tripping you up, where you'll need to duck to avoid the poison dart booby traps. Eventually, the beast won't be able to catch you; finally, the chicken breast is spicy and tender.

Conversely, the educational labyrinth that is skateboarding cannot and will not ever end. Every pathway contains a minotaur. Sometimes you can tame them (learning kickflips), but they will never all truly be defeated (I still regularly eat shit on kickflips after 23 years of doing them). That's part of what makes skateboarding so exciting — its potential and unpredictability. The unknown becomes known in a swift, sometimes brutal manner.

When I first witnessed skateboarding, it was confounding. Then my older brother took it up, and it became something I needed to figure out immediately. I poured through what limited magazines and videos I could find, as if they were an operating manual. For a while, *Pro Skater* filled that void. Child-me could do the tricks in-game that I couldn't execute or even understand in real life. Then I began to recognize the names of maneuvers from the game in the pages of *Transworld Skateboarding* that covered the walls of my brother's and, later, my rooms. What were once abstract images began to take on definition.

When prolonged Northern Albertan winters finally retreated, I'd push my much-too-large-for-me skateboard down our street, riding up and down the rounded sidewalk curbs, pretending they were a personal half-pipe outside our home. I'd imagine myself doing the 540 tailgrabs I'd just spent the morning making my Chad Muska avatar do — a trick the IRL Muska couldn't land either. The heelflips that would eventually skewer me in the driveway were possible on the screen. I could heelflip down stairs, onto rails, over cars, simply by pressing right + square. Eventually, I'd begin to land them in the driveway. These skateboarding tricks made their way from magazines and videos to a video game before finding themselves, after great struggle, under my feet.

This method was slow but effective and generally went as such: after school, I'd go home and eat a snack (some rotation of peanut butter on a spoon, plain mustard squirted onto a cold all-beef wiener, a can of uncooked Chef Boyardee Ravioli) and watch the tail end of *Judge Judy* before *The Simpsons* came on channel 31 (Fox Rochester). After that, I'd push in my brother's *Fulfill the Dream* VHS and watch the sections with Steve Olson and Aaron Snyder and Toan Nguyen and Sammy Baptista, then skate to my rural Albertan hometown's charmingly basic skatepark (which consisted of a rectangular concrete pad dotted with several hollow steel obstacles that, every time you rode on them, rang out across the neighboring hockey rink and playground like two ship hulls colliding) and try to learn a new trick. If I couldn't, once home that evening, I'd try to make sense of it by doing it repeatedly in various levels of *Pro Skater*.

As small and pixelated as they were, those levels also served as new worlds to explore as I lived in my own limited reality. It was a way to experience locales and skate spots I could only encounter in videos and magazines — an interactive stopgap until I was able to skate them in real life. "Warehouse," the level featured in the *Pro Skater* Pizza Hut demo disk that helped ignite the game's buzz, was akin to my home skatepark. Basic, lacking flow, but still a place where I'd spend hours practicing tricks with no complaints. "School," a level based in Miami, Florida, is comparatively expansive. You spawn on the roof of a covered walkway and fling yourself to the campus below to start the level. Then stairs, handrails, benches, and picnic tables await you — all the things my alma mater, Central Elementary School, did not have. Here I could skate outside in presumably muggy Floridian heat while I actually sat in my basement, heat cranked against a −35 degree Celsius Albertan winter.

The "Mall" level, well, as far as even pretend malls go, this one was admittedly underwhelming. As a child, I'd take weekend trips into *the city* with my father, one of our stops always being the crown jewel of the Prairies, West Edmonton Mall. So, I knew malls, and this wasn't it. Where were the rollercoasters, Hooters restaurants, pirate ships, dolphins, submarines, and giant brass whales whose cavernous mouths you could stroll inside of? This very real mall was more preposterous than the one onscreen.

Contest levels like "Skatepark," "Burnside," and "Roswell," where you competed against the game's other characters to see who could land the highest score, were my least favorites. Even though I was the only one applying it, I found the competitive pressure too tense, sucking the enjoyment out of the game. A few years later, I'd enter my first real-life skateboarding competition in Nanaimo, BC, and endure much of the same feeling.

My favorite levels were those like "Downtown," a supposed approximation of Minneapolis, Minnesota. That was what I dreamed Lac La Biche could be. A city center teeming with obstacles, one after the other. I would often create narratives for my onscreen avatar, pretending I was cruising around the level to film tricks for my video part, like the ones in the skate videos I watched incessantly. My daydreaming was most effective here and in "Streets," a crude rendering of San Francisco that was essentially an amalgam of all the city's most famous attractions and skate spots (including Lombard Street, streetcars, Hubba Hideout, and one of skateboarding's most influential locales, EMB, or Embarcadero, where a defining generation of skateboarding icons honed their skills and stoked their legends). I could do tricks down Hubba Hideout, the same ledge Steve Olson backside tailslide shoved in the *Fulfill the Dream* video. If I wanted, I could even one-up him by *kickflipping* into the tailside.

This constant state of visualization, from a child playing video games to an adult eyeing up an embankment on the side of a building to see if it's skateable, is one of the more formative aspects of skateboarding. It can lend itself to the conceptualization and execution of tricks, poems, cabinetry, and even, when necessary, escape.

Because, in essence, and trite summation, that's what video games are: an escape. From the everyday slog, the homework you have a deep aversion to touching, that relationship you haven't figured out how to mend, the depression you don't quite have the tools to contend with. Of course, video games are also fun; an escape doesn't always mean you're running away or being pursued. You can escape into the alternating timelines of a doomed Earth-like realm for a few hours (*Chrono Trigger*, 1995, Square) because it simply rules. They can be mindless, violent timewasters like *Duke Nukem* (3D Realms, 1991) or fully interactive art pieces with engaging, challenging storylines like *Disco Elysium* (ZA/UM, 2019).

Video games have been all those things for me. *Pro Skater* and its many iterations throughout the years served multiple roles. Teacher, time killer, refuge. In middle school, as pre-teen angst swirled with what I'd now in retrospect recognize as regular periods of depression, I'd bury myself in *Pro Skater 3* (Neversoft, 2001), escaping to those locales I deeply wished my skateboard and I could travel to. In an effort to escape the harsh Albertan climate, I'd move to the Kootenays in the mountains of British Columbia with my father for high school. The following winter, my stepfather would die from a cruel and prolonged bout of cancer, and the only way I knew how to grieve was by losing myself in skateboarding and video games. *Tony Hawk's Underground* (*THUG*; Neversoft, 2003) was where I put my energy when I wasn't skating in the unfinished basement, watching skate videos, shoveling the driveway, or letting my grades circle the toilet basin.

THUG, unlike previous entries in the *Pro Skater* franchise, has a narrative. First, you, the player, create a custom avatar before beginning your journey as a young skater with hopes of becoming a professional. Of course, at 15, 16 years old, that was exactly what I wanted to do, this game serving as a simulator for a life I wanted to live if I wasn't trapped in the snow-capped valleys of the Kootenays. Perhaps it was all the weed I'd been smoking, but I even remember feeling a little knot of sorrow and rage tighten in my chest when your in-game best friend, Eric Sparrow, who you start on your adventure to pro-dom with, (spoiler) betrays you to advance his own career. How could Sparrow do that to his *best friend*?

Such is the power of a video game: dispelling and igniting any range of emotions through the furious mashing of buttons.

It wasn't long after finishing *THUG* that I began a nearly 15-year hiatus from video games. It wasn't a conscious decision to abstain; real-life skateboarding had fully taken over my life. After high school, I'd move to Vancouver to skateboard and ostensibly pursue some type of post-secondary education. The only games I played at the time were the *New York Times* crossword app and the will-they-won't-they of whether I'd find a silverfish crawling in my bed. It wouldn't be until March 2020, when a strange virus inched its way closer and lockdowns loomed, that I hustled to my local Best Buy and made my most important purchase of the last three years: a Nintendo Switch.

During the months of uncertainty that followed, ones mainly spent in my small bachelor suite apartment, I'd spend hours touring around a vast Hyrule Kingdom while playing *The Legend of Zelda: Breath of the Wild* (Nintendo, 2017). Riding horses through tall grasses, climbing mountains to peer out over stunning vistas, padding barefoot along white-sand beaches, and occasionally grappling with the forces of an absolute, generational evil that had returned to paralyze and destroy the known world — these were regular parts of my evening escape. When I could stop refreshing the news and worrying about a future I couldn't control, I focused on the one I could. The only thing I had to worry about in Hyrule was if my goddamn sword would break mid-battle again.

Eventually, and tentatively, I'd start to go outside again, but I'd keep playing video games. My relationship with them is now less urgent, but the ability to get lost inside of one is no less potent. In the nearly two decades away from the world of video games, the games themselves advanced at a rapid clip, from graphics to gameplay to storytelling and beyond. What I'd known as an angst-addled teenager pales in the face of what's on the market today. The visceral hesitancy I have at the thought of joining a 30-person lobby to play a first-person shooter online makes me feel indescribably, irreparably old. A labyrinth I choose not to enter. An unknown that can stay unknown.

I can still get out of video games what *Pro Skater* provided to my various stages of youth: a getaway, an entrance, an education. And I can appreciate it as a space I was able to find

7

The World Drops In

The unprecedented success of *Pro Skater* is often credited with
kickstarting a sea change in skateboarding, inspiring new generations of skateboarders, legitimizing the sport in the eyes
of everyone from sports fans to public officials, and allowing
skateboarders to workshop once-impossible tricks onscreen
before taking them out into the streets. Hawk himself sub-
scribes to all of this, explaining in *Pretending I'm a Superman:
The Tony Hawk Video Game Story*, "The generation that grew
up playing *THPS* and started skating because of it thought that
360 flip to crooked grind is just something you do when you
learn to skate, and that shit didn't even exist when I grew up . . .
if you looked today at the kind of tricks that people are putting on video and doing in contests, it's *THPS* stuff. I'm sorry
[laughs], but that is where it came from."

73

American pro skateboarder Kevin Kowalski cites his copy of *Pro Skater* as a defining first exposure to skateboarding. Rising British skateboarding prospect Jordan Thackery from Norfolk, England, told the *Guardian* that his grandparents buying him the game prompted him to beg his mum for a board. Granted, this is just anecdotal international influence, but it shouldn't be discounted. These are stories that most skaters from the initial *Pro Skater* generation have either heard or lived. Geoff Rowley tried to deconstruct that appeal, saying that the *Pro Skater* franchise helped show the world how cool skateboarding could be, giving it the necessary nudge to plant itself firmly in the mainstream.

With all that in mind, did *Pro Skater* lead to skateboarding's turn-of-the-millennium rise, and can it be credited with its current ubiquity? Perhaps. It even seems likely. But can it be proved? Are there reams of data points to sift through and dots to connect that will illustrate how this iconic video game took from, shaped, and then steered an entire culture? Not really. But if you look at the limited sources available, from hard stats to anecdotes, there was a clear shift following the release of *Pro Skater*. Skateboarding's popularity, if charted on a line graph, was once a shaky and inconsistent thing with a y-axis full of dramatic peaks and valleys. But it began to steady as the 2000s clambered on, all inclines and brief plateaus. So, what are the loose metrics that can measure those gains?

When attempting to trace the global growth of skateboarding, one has to look at the development of the skateboarding industry and the many companies producing the variety of hard and soft goods that skateboarders worldwide need to participate in their shared obsession. To do this, one must rely on a series of terms like market size, market share, end-user, trend analysis, product insights, and segment forecasts. The purity of riding a skateboard down the sidewalk, that feeling of freedom as cracks *clack-clack* underneath your feet, also depends on our merciless capitalist constructs.

If we follow the number of sales, regional market growth, anecdotal evidence, and the general populace's awareness of skateboarding over time, we can make a case for where skateboarding stands size-wise. Because it has grown, skateboarding currently has more participants and is more popular than ever. It isn't a stretch to say the release of *Pro Skater* in 1999 is partly responsible for that rise. Tony Hawk believes so, saying in *Pretending I'm a Superman*, "Skateboarding became bigger than Little League, truly. America's pastime had been surpassed by skateboarding at that time, and definitely, the video game was a huge factor in that."

It's a statement that's hard to dispute. The game was a Trojan horse, entering the homes of millions worldwide, exposing kids, teenagers, their parents, and more to this gamified version of skateboarding. Admittedly, there's not a lot of available data to follow here, but to draw the first few lines on our line graph, we look to a handful of stats compiled by the International Association of Skateboard Companies (IASC), an organization whose primary goal was to stimulate the growth of skateboarding. Established in 1995, IASC described itself as "a diverse group of skateboard manufacturers, distributors, contest organizers, private skateparks, and individuals . . . [whose mission] is to represent the global skateboarding community with a united voice by listening, understanding and acting on the needs of skateboarders and the skateboard industry. "

IASC's major initiative was Go Skateboarding Day, an annual event held on June 21 in cities around the world to promote its namesake. The organization encouraged and helped local brands and distributors put on community-oriented events that generally include skaters traveling in large, rolling mobs around their respective locales. In Vancouver, BC, the city's viaduct connecting Chinatown to Downtown is a mainstay of the event's yearly route, skateboarders swelling and congesting the entirety of the overpass. It is at once a beautiful and overwhelming sight. The first time I joined the throngs over a decade ago, it was an introduction to just how vast and connected the skateboarding community could be. Hundreds of us swarming for a single, simple purpose: to skate some shit.

In 2001, IASC shared some key figures they'd put together about the state of the skateboarding industry at the time. These numbers, released just a couple of years following the launch of *Pro Skater*, stated that there were 16 million skateboarders in the United States and more than 20 million internationally (including the U.S.). Using data gathered from around 300 different manufacturers of skateboards and skateboard-related products, it appeared that the industry had amassed US$1.4 billion in annual retail sales. And even with skateboarding primarily taking place in the streets in the early aughts, there were around 800 public and private skateparks in the U.S.

Now, going by a market analysis released by an organization called Grand View Research, the global skateboard market size sat around US$2 billion in value in 2020 and is expected to rise to US$2.4 billion by 2025. That's a nearly 72% projected increase in under two-and-a-half decades. Other data shows that the number of skateboarders in the U.S. dipped to 8.9 million in 2020, and there's an oft-repeated figure claiming that the global number of skateboarders had ballooned to a staggering 85 million. Are any of those participant numbers accurate? Ballpark? What we do know is that the industry continues to grow along with increased awareness and presence of skateboarding in popular culture.

CULTURAL FOOTPRINT

From the X Games elevating competitive skating to a national audience, to *Pro Skater* grabbing that baton to bring it into the homes and lives of untold millions, to the international cultural phenomenon of *Jackass* (which starred pro skater Bam

Margera) bursting out of the offices of the terminally irreverent skateboarding magazine *Big Brother*, to hit MTV reality shows built around pro skateboarders like Ryan Sheckler and Rob Dyrdek, to skateboarders securing sponsorship deals with corporate behemoths like Nike, Adidas, Target, Mountain Dew, Red Bull, and Monster, to Louis Vuitton launching a line of skate shoes — skateboarding is now comfortably in the collective consciousness.

That's without even mentioning skateboarding's global breakthrough moment, when in 2016 — much to the dismay of the "hardcores" who felt the soul of skateboarding was in peril, and to the extreme delight of organizers and industry leaders — skateboarding was confirmed as a new sport for the Tokyo 2020 Olympics. Approximately 15.3 million people watched Japan's Momiji Nishiya take gold in the inaugural women's street skateboarding event, and this new platform created superstars overnight. Team USA's Jagger Eaton earned bronze in the men's street skateboarding event and in short order found himself on Jimmy Kimmel's late-night set. Yuto Horigome, who took gold ahead of Eaton, has risen through the ranks of celebrity in Japan, gracing the covers of magazines, scoring high-profile advertisement campaigns with non-skateboarding-related companies like the multinational information technology and electronics corporation NEC, and even meeting (via Zoom) with the Prime Minister of Japan. Rayssa Leal, the 14-year-old who took silver behind Nishiya, has become a hero in her native Brazil, booking appearances at schools around the country, starring in features for *Vogue Brasil*, and having her Instagram following swell to nearly 6.5 million in the span of a few weeks. This level of notoriety was once a very lonely place in the world of skateboarding, belonging singularly to one man, Tony Hawk (who, as of writing this, has just over 7 million Instagram followers).

Skateboarding's involvement in the Olympics has offered more than individual fame and endorsement deals; it's conveyed to federal and local officials that this once-maligned pastime is a legitimate sporting endeavor. As a result, governments around the world are now funding Olympic *skateboarding*. Sure, this is a sterilized, made-for-TV version of it, but it's still a remarkable shift from skateboarding's somewhat ballyhooed rebellious origins and legacy. The years of sneaking into and draining backyard swimming pools now butt up against a present where local municipalities champion the construction and proliferation of skateparks. Following the completion of a new skatepark on Gabriola Island in British Columbia in May 2022, local politician Doug Routley said that the space "provides a challenge to users in a safe environment that's a gathering place for people in the community. It's our privilege to work with the federal government, Regional District of Nanaimo and community fundraisers to enhance recreational options on Gabriola Island." Skateboarding's public-image journey from nuisance to government-endorsed recreational option is stark. And that increase in public skateboarding infrastructure contributes to the story of skateboarding's growth overall.

In that 2001 update, IASC claimed there were roughly 800 public and private skateparks in the United States. In

2019, The Skatepark Project identified roughly 2,800 public skateparks throughout the country and estimated that there are about 700 more they had yet to identify. If these numbers are accurate, that's a 337.5% increase in the number of city-sanctioned destinations for skateboarders in the United States alone. The injection of mainstream legitimacy given to skateboarding following its inclusion in the Olympics will likely only encourage more municipal governments to earmark money for quarters pipes and manual pads, along with baseball diamonds and basketball courts.

Now, visualize the Domino Effect meme with the guy in the pleated slacks pushing a small domino into a line of progressively bigger dominoes. Let's say that *Pro Skater* is the small domino and the Olympics are the nipple-high one at the end, knocked over by the growing ripples of impactful moments spurred by *Pro Skater*'s successes. Is it possible that this incredibly popular video game is what sparked skateboarding's rise to cultural and economic import around the world? Did the clarion call of Goldfinger's John Feldmann singing about his arrested development as the player's digital avatar struggled to smash through five mall directories help transform generations of potential Little Leaguers into skateboarders? Was this when the uncaring were suddenly swayed into giving a shit about skateboarding? The first step in bringing it from backyard ramps and back alleys into the gleaming, heavily restricted broadcast material library of the IOC and NBC?

After growing up as one of a handful of skateboarders in a rural Albertan town in the late '90s to skating amongst a

Pro Skater > Olympic skateboarding?

sea of fellow skaters as we took over major thoroughfares in Vancouver ten years later to being part of a worldwide audience of millions watching Olympic skateboarding events on my television another decade on, I'd say, yeah, probably. And it's been a bit complicated to square that growth away internally. To go from being teased for riding a skateboard to seeing it venerated on the world stage and become a (sometimes literal) fashion accessory has been uncanny and a bit maddening to watch. Pop culture descends on and devours the niche and the trending with little remorse, like the genuine angst of grunge that was defanged and marketed with haste or the high-flying theatrics of '80s vert skateboarding that were packaged for mass consumption as banal youth fad. Could skateboarding survive that again? Would James, Nathan, and the other outsiders have found refuge in skateboarding if it was as popular as it is today? It's difficult to say, but I'd posit that no matter how big skateboarding gets, so much of it is subjective and experiential that its status in the public eye can't change the base appeal that has hooked the millions who have stepped on a board: that riding one feels like magic, a nightmare, and often both at once.

8

Franchise and Fall from Grace

Whether it is bocce, paragliding, accounting, or cello — being good at something is generally, as a rule, quite hard. It takes untold hours of practice and resolve to become good at a thing you are initially bad at. To note: "good" is not mastery of a craft. Good is a step or two above competent. A level of ability where you're not just treading water but cutting through it with a growing sense of grace. Improving upon that takes serious and uncommon dedication. A committed, all-consuming passion that eventually, if all goes well, translates into deft creativity that appears effortless but, in reality, is the culmination of a lifetime of work.

Most people do find a thing and become good at it. The trickiest part about being good at something, mind you, is staying good at it. It's not like a forklift ticket or credit card with expiry dates that require a simple bit of paperwork to renew; maintaining goodness demands constant goodness to be performed. If you want, think about Bob Dylan. He's put out nearly 40 albums, and for a time, most of those albums were pretty good. Then some of them weren't. Eventually, seven albums and nearly a decade would pass between the double-platinum-selling *Blonde on Blonde* and *Blood on the Tracks*, with chaff making up most of that space and what would follow, including 2009's universally panned novelty album *Christmas in the Heart*. "All the eggnog at Santa's workshop couldn't impair me enough to willingly listen to *Christmas in the Heart* again, despite Dylan donating all his royalties to several charities. I'd rather just cut them a check directly," *Consequence of Sound* would say of the album. Because being good and consistently good are two distinctly difficult things to execute in tandem, even for titans in their respective mediums like Bob Dylan.

THE (GOOD, GREAT, MEH, AND BAD) TONYS

When *Tony Hawk's Pro Skater* was released in 1999, it set an unexpectedly high bar for the team at Neversoft. *IGN* gave it a 9.8/10, *GameSpot* gave it a 9.3/10, and *Electric Playground* beamed that while "it may be a little too daunting for anyone other than hardcore gamers and/or boarders, otherwise, *Tony Hawk's Pro Skater* might very well be the perfect video game." *The perfect video game*. That glowing response for *Pro Skater* was stunning and somewhat unexpected, catching its developers off guard. It was a surprise, in part because that first game was a bit of a rush job that left the team without time to implement important and obvious aspects to the game, like manuals (the balancing of the skateboard on solely the front or rear wheels), a fundamental category of skateboarding trick that was introduced in the game's sequel. There was also a push to involve motion capture in the game design. While they had Hawk strap on full-body tights covered with little plastic balls and fly around a vert ramp performing trick after trick in order to bring a higher level of physical accuracy to the game, the team ran out of time to implement all the data they'd collected. Hawk's balled-up efforts were a wash, which is why all the characters in *Pro Skater* move with a similar stiffness.

Slight setbacks aside, Neversoft made a very good thing on the first try, which is, as noted previously, hard to do. It's also harder to continue doing. But their team took the lessons learned from *Pro Skater*, refined them, and in less than a year after the release of the original, launched *Tony Hawk's Pro Skater 2* (2000). The sequel would eclipse its predecessor in sales[14] and critical reception with gamers and skateboarders alike, with *IGN* and *GameSpot* giving a rating of 9.9/10 and *CNET* bestowing it a perfect 10/10, along with calling it "the best skateboarding game ever and one of the greatest

14 *Pro Skater* was the third-highest-selling video game in the United States in 1999, and *Pro Skater 2* would land at number two the following year. The third-best-selling game of 2000? *Pro Skater*.

PlayStation games of all time." Hawk would even cite it as his favorite of the series, as would most of my childhood friends in between bites of Fruit Roll-Ups.

The resounding success of the first two games in the *Pro Skater* series would kickstart one of the most storied sports video game franchises in history, with 20 separate titles released over two decades. *Pro Skater 3* (2001) would continue this history of overall goodness, with critics showering it in 9s and the occasional 10/10. While Elissa Steamer would remain the only woman character in the game, for the first time, the create-a-skater function in *Pro Skater 3* allowed players to customize their own female-coded avatars. *Jackass* star and medium-sized sensation Bam Margera was also added as a playable character to the game, alongside unlockable options like Wolverine, Darth Maul, and the space marine from *Doom*; all signs *Pro Skater* was further entrenching itself into the infinite, enigmatic arms of pop culture.

Pro Skater 4 (2002) moved away from the restrictive two-minute time limit that defined the game's "career mode" in its previous iterations, allowing players to explore levels at their leisure and interact with non-playable characters to activate challenges and progress through the game. Subsequent games would each offer some sort of technical advancements, from new mechanics like powersliding (where the skateboarder pushes their board 90 degrees and slides on all four wheels) to skitching (holding on to the back of a vehicle while on a skateboard) to adding in fleshed-out narratives for the player to follow, like with *Tony Hawk's Underground*

(*THUG*; 2003), *THUG* 2 (2004), and *Tony Hawk's American Wasteland* (2005).

Despite these somewhat consistent innovations, the series reached a critical plateau with *THUG*, barely hanging on to its comfortable 9s with some reviewers and slipping into the 8s with others. *THUG* 2 and *American Wasteland* fell further, the latter dipping to a 6.9 in a less-than-kind *GameSpot* review. The game's original magic had begun to fade — that inescapable struggle of being good and being consistent finally catching up with it. The name value and memories made over countless hours of gameplay in early iterations of the series could still pull in some players, but its grip on them was loosening. Its old tricks were becoming repetitive, the new ones it tried coming too late and with a whiff of desperation.

An *IGN* review of *THUG* 2 distilled this effect as "Neversoft's hurl-everything-you-can-in-a-last-ditch-effort in the hope to create something new. The effort, while recognized, is an example of a series that in many ways has perhaps run out of steam and good ideas, and fans of the series are likely to respond with a mixed reaction of disappointment and excitement, while grumpily trudging to the store to buy it anyway." That's how it tends to go with these sorts of offerings, whether it's video games, music, movies, or television. Most of us have made that grim trudge to pay witness to a thing you've become invested in but whose later installments you would regret taking in (*Game of Thrones*, season 8).

Things wouldn't get better for the *Pro Skater* series. Scrolling down the aggregate review scores for the seven subsequent installments that launched between 2006 and 2014, including *Tony Hawk's Downhill Jam*, *Tony Hawk's Project 8*, *Tony Hawk's Proving Ground*, *Tony Hawk's Motion*, *Tony Hawk: Ride*, *Tony Hawk: Shred*, and *Tony Hawk's Pro Skater HD*, reveals a perilous decline across all consoles. Scores touched as high as 81% (*Project 8* on the Xbox 360) before falling to catastrophic, subterranean lows of 44% (*Ride* on the PlayStation 3). *Proving Ground* was the last title Neversoft worked on, and though their product had lost its luster, once the game shifted hands to producer Robomodo for the *Ride*, *Shred*, and *Pro Skater HD* titles, the drop in quality was precipitous. The former two games utilize a roundly panned skateboard-shaped controller that the player stands on to pilot their avatar and do tricks on screen. It's a frustrating, less than intuitive contraption that I once spent a drunken evening at a friend's yelling at, wishing I could, for the love of god, just fucking skate.

Shred brought in a meagre 3,000 units in its first week of total U.S. sales, leading to Robomodo laying off nearly 60 staff members and being taken off the *Pro Skater* series by Activision. It was a tough but understandable call that Activision would backtrack on shortly after by giving the producer the reins of *Pro Skater HD* and its follow-up that is considered the game's death knell: *Tony Hawk's Pro Skater 5*. Technically the 18th game in the series, *Entertainment Weekly* dubbed it the "Worst Video Game of 2015," a sentiment shared by the majority of critics, *Eurogamer* calling *Pro Skater 5* "glitch-ridden and seemingly unfinished . . . a tragic swansong for Tony Hawk's video game career." That would become a reality for some —

Robomodo shuttered just under a year after the dramatic failure of their final *Pro Skater* offering. Hawk's licensing deal with Activision would eventually expire and not be renewed, putting the game on an indefinite hiatus.

It was an ignominious last attempt, a rush job to finish a game before deadline and the expiration of the *Pro Skater* license, a blatant cash grab and a clear failure of imagination. The formula that made the original and the first few of its sequels so successful was still mostly there; it'd just become tired. And instead of taking the time to evolve the franchise in any meaningful way, the developers had no choice but to acquiesce to their near yearly deadlines, popping out installment after installment, the game's inherent appeal dulling with each. This decline in goodness and consistency also left an opening for another problem to arise for the series: competitors.

THE MARKET EXPANDS

Skate, developed by EA Black Box and published by Electronic Arts, was released in September 2007. A move away from the arcade-style of *Pro Skater* and verging into something of a skateboarding simulator, *Skate* received mixed but mostly positive reviews. *IGN* scored it an 8.8/10, and the *New York Times* acknowledged some of the game's hiccups but said for a first effort "it is rare to find a game that comes so close to doing everything right." *Skate* even received the Best Individual Sports Game award at the now-defunct Video Game Awards, beating out competitors *Tiger Woods PGA Tour 08*, *Virtua Tennis*, and *Tony Hawk's Proving Ground*.

Set in the expansive fictional city of San Vanelona (a portmanteau of noted skateboarding destinations San Francisco, Vancouver, and Barcelona), you pilot your avatar around its streets and do tricks using the game's signature Flickit controls, which utilize the joysticks and the various ways you can push, pull, and flick them to execute maneuvers. Unlike *Pro Skater*, where there was a button to ollie and another to grind an incoming handrail; in *Skate*, the player pulls back on the right joystick to ollie and aims their board with the other in the position and type of grind they want to land in on said incoming handrail.

While a more intuitive system, it also proved to be more difficult to master — which gamers and skaters loved. And across two more installments in the form of *Skate 2* and *Skate 3*, the product only became more refined (*Skate 3* initially had a notable number of bugs that inspired a whole genre of YouTube video where vloggers seek out and make compilations of the game's glitches.) *Skate*'s success would run in stark contrast to *Pro Skater*'s ragged drop off the x-axis of goodness and lead many to believe that the mantle of best skateboarding game had officially been passed. This, despite the fact the *Skate* series only released three titles between 2007 and 2010. (A new game, *skate.*, was announced by Electronic Arts and developer Full Circle in 2020 but has yet to be released as of writing.) A quick, striking impact comparable to *Pro Skater*'s first few years on the market. That success, one could argue, was strengthened by the genre's biggest name. The market created by *Pro Skater* and the untold number of new skateboarders it inspired undoubtedly funneled into *Skate*. It was an audience that had become more closely aligned with core skateboarding and was searching for a more true-to-life skating experience, beyond the arcade-y vision of *Pro Skater*.

Something of a cult favorite, *Skate 3* would even return to UK bestseller lists in 2020, a decade after its original release, when it was put on sale on Xbox Live. Such is the power the game still wields. Other skateboarding titles would launch in the vacuum left by the *Skate* series and *Pro Skater*'s decline. Games like *Skater XL* (Easy Day Studios, 2020) and *Session* (Crea-ture Studios, 2019) would pick up where *Skate* left off, creating simulators with a much higher level of difficulty along with advanced replay systems so players can record and piece together their own video parts, much like skateboarders do in real life. *Session* even allows players to add a VX1000 filter to their captured clips, mimicking the camera style and silhouette of the Sony VX1000, a video camera with a much-beloved aesthetic in the world of skateboarding.

These are games designed with core skateboarders in mind, a relatively niche market. One that likely wouldn't exist without its predecessor in *Pro Skater*. Because that game proved an essential monetary truth: people will buy skateboarding video games — a lot of them. When the quality in *Pro Skater*'s releases dipped over the years, part of that audience it built craved something more, creating an opening for these competitors. *Skate* filled the void and became the premier option until indie games like *Session* and *Skater XL* joined in nearly a decade later.

But even in that underserved market of AAA skateboarding titles, there was life teeming below the surface. There were games that strayed far from the path of realism, indie titles like *SkateBIRD* (Glass Bottom Games, 2021) where you, a bird, skate around on a fingerboard in a human-sized world; the side-scrolling action platformer series *OlliOlli* (roll7, 2014–present) that takes place in a surreal neon, cartoony environment full of bizarre and adorable characters; and even mobile offerings cropped up, like *True Skate* (True Axis, 2012), which boldly touts itself as the "#1 game in 80 countries. Loved by skaters all over the world."

Another title even looked toward an alternate future. *PERFECT STRIDE* was to be a first-person, postapocalyptic skateboarding video game by independent developers Arcane Kids. In 2013, they asked what would've happened "if in 1999 Tony Hawk didn't land the 900?" Unfortunately, the answer appears to be catastrophic flooding, the cessation of our planet's normal understanding of gravity, and the rise of an immortal Time Wizard after Hawk was unable to "[trigger] an explosion of corporate skateboarding."

In regards to the latter, Ben Esposito from Arcane Kids would tell *Polygon*, "So, after Tony Hawk did not land the 900 at the 1999 X-Games, it set forth the course of events that allowed . . . a Time Wizard to come into power. He himself is immortal, so he prevents everyone else from dying . . . He wishes for death, but he can't [die], so he reigns over the world so that [other] people can't die." Alright.

The goal of the game? "Well, there's rumors that there's one bullet left on earth," Russell Honor of Arcane Kids explained in the same interview with *Polygon*, "and so your mission is to try and find that bullet so that you can kill the Time Wizard." One assumes that would also free humanity, because eventually immortality becomes a prison that one must escape, for it is not living but merely existing. And what better way to bring yourself closer to a life than by skateboarding?

PERFECT STRIDE would never be fully completed or released, but an unfinished version of the game is free to download from the Internet Archive. And while its concept may be a bit out there and convoluted, it's an interesting example of another skateboarding game taking a swing at commentary on the success and industry-changing impact of *Pro Skater*. Due to the catastrophic disarray in the world of *PERFECT STRIDE*, one assumes that not only did society crumble when Hawk failed to land the 900, but *Pro Skater*, skateboarding, and its corporate interests also went down with it. Commercial success, of course, being the only thing keeping civilization together.

Clearly, the desire to play skateboarding games was there, even if the market for AAA titles had cooled off. YouTubers and Twitch streamers with a focus on skateboarding and skateboarding video games recognized this and started to deliver content to a hungry audience base. Garrett Ginner, a YouTuber with over 750,000 subscribers who follow his weekly escapades in videos like "Street Skating in LA With Friends!," "Skating over my new car!," and "I broke the new car . . . ," also has a dedicated gaming channel, Garrett Ginner Gaming, with over 128,000 subscribers. In these videos, Ginner plays mostly skateboarding games, comparing and contrasting *Session* and *Skater XL* for tens of thousands of views.

ZexyZek, a YouTuber with over 2.5 million subscribers, still publishes *Skate 3* related videos over a decade after the game's original release. "EPIC SKATE 3 CHALLENGES!," a 2017 installment in a series where ZexyZek performs viewer-suggested stunts in the game, has a whopping 24 million views. Among those millions of viewers is a mélange of gamers and skaters, all pining for content, and for more skateboarding video games where more of that content can come from.

Then, in 2020, Tony Hawk decided to take another stab at the whole video game thing. The medium had defined his career and launched him out of skateboarding's bubble and firmly into stardom, but the market had changed and what *Pro Skater* had become was no longer what players wanted. So instead of adding another roman numeral to the pile that had begun to fester, Activision decided to return to something they knew people had loved for over two decades.

9

Tony's Magic Touch

Every few months, Tony Hawk will trend on Twitter. Usually, it's because he's shared an anecdote that goes viral of a stranger asking if he knows that he looks just like Tony Hawk — an occurrence so common it's become its own meme. Other times, it's because Hawk is struggling to land a skateboarding trick that he pioneered in his youth, tearily claiming to the camera that it will be the last time he'll do it as he climbs further into his 50s.

These bits acknowledge a self-perceived liminal space that Hawk exists in, somewhere between the successes of his athletic prime, the celebrity it garnered him, and the disconnect of a life without the abilities that built and defined it. They are also clearly social media brand-building exercises, but if you look at your timeline long enough and bring your face right up to the screen, you'll see seams of truth: these are pieces of midlife performance art. A way for his present self to contend with the past and recognize what future may lie ahead (and sell some skincare lotion along the way). Like Tom Cruise doing his own stunts well into his fifth decade of life in sequel after sequel, his limits are acknowledged, the environment is controlled, and we eat it up.

A cursory scroll through Hawk's Twitter feed makes one thing clear: he's still an incredibly prolific product marketer. Promotions with GoDaddy, Crash Bandicoot, and Pacifico dot his profile in the first few months of 2021 alone. It's a testament to his near-universal appeal that he can represent brands and products across such a wide-ranging selection of industries. They're the monetized proof of Hawk's permanence in popular culture. A 2017 cameo on *Whose Line Is It Anyway?* on YouTube is just a few flicks of the finger away from a two-decade-old stunt on MTV's *Senseless Acts of Video*.

In these clips, we see Hawk as what he became to the masses in the late '90s: the archetypal skateboarder with a southern Californian lilt. He's remained skateboarding's primary cultural touchpoint and its most popular name. His iconic video game franchise helped push him to that point of ubiquity, but his landing of the first-ever 900 at the X Games that same year is what solidified his credentials to the layperson. It was a uniquely captivating sporting moment that made sense to the uninitiated watching at home: he'd spun around in the air on a skateboard more times than anyone else in the world ever had or could before. Which proved he was the absolute best person at doing this thing, because how could it not? If you watched the euphoric crowd rush Hawk in the bottom of the half-pipe after he landed the trick, it was undeniable.

In the decades since, Hawk has done everything there is to do in the career of a professional skateboarder and light-years more. He's owned his own companies, promoted cars and Bagel Bites, guest-starred on an episode of *The Simpsons*, become a meme, and has continued to innovate on his skate-board right into his 50s. Judging by his online presence, he seems to be in a good place. And why shouldn't he be? You'd hope finding such a singular success would have that effect.

It would also put his efforts at retiring tricks from his past into context — it's a lot easier to mourn when you have your life in order. When Hawk did his last documented 900 at 48 years old, it was an unofficial send-off to the particular twisting of a body from which an entire personal industry bloomed. Then the odometer ticked past 50. His self-proclaimed "last ever" ollie 540 that he landed at 52 years old in March 2021? That was a funeral. When Hawk finally rode away, it was like he'd placed the body in the casket himself. The history and emotions attached to the maneuver were evident as he collapsed to his knees and wept. "Happy I made it" the trick's fitting eulogy.

But, it should be noted that these are ultimately retire-ments Hawk himself is declaring. He's not being ushered out the door with a gold watch by the company. Who's to say he can't do another grabless 540 at 54? We have to take his word.

There are other tricks he's exhumed, acknowledging that he might leave them propped up in a chair wearing sunglasses until it's time to play with them again.

"Did this trick once 10 years ago and just did it again today for the second time. No finality to it, more like visiting an old friend . . . or a scary acquaintance," Hawk tweeted after doing a bluntslide to fakie over the channel in his personal half-pipe, just days after the retirement of the ollie 540. It must be hard to contend with the limits of your own mortality when you continue to push back on them every day, when the limits are ever-changing and mostly self-imposed. Especially when those same physical abilities you're cordoning off are what helped you become who you are and how you pay your bills. Like the aged boxer who lays their gloves in the center of the ring, only to put them back on to fight months or years later, can you walk forward into the future denying the thing that gave your life purpose, even if that thing reminds you every day that it's moved on?

Hawk knows that physically he's almost out of season, which is why he's picking and choosing what ornaments to take off the tree first, starting with the star and working his way down. And if you're making the effort to tell the public that these are your last attempts, why not make a show of it? Hawk even tried to commemorate the upcoming retirement of tricks like the Varial 5, Gymnast Plant, Magic Dance, Front Side Cab, and Finger Flip by creating a series of custom Last Trick NFTs, or non-fungible tokens, essentially a digital trading card that is sold as belonging uniquely to the buyer thanks to its code being stowed away in the blockchain as proof of ownership. This was a move roundly criticized by those in the skateboarding community and beyond who are rightly skeptical of the grifty nature of NFTs. It was a rare misstep by Hawk in a mostly squeaky clean public-facing career. As he's aged he has simply become more beloved, falling into the role of something like a fatherly figure within popular culture — kind, supportive, and just sort of always there. He's arrived at a level of notoriety in his life where every sighting and move he makes carries the possibility of becoming a story.

In 2017, Hawk made the news for being amongst a crowd of bystanders filming a car engulfed by flames in Manhattan's Lower East Side. The car's owner was at the scene and got a selfie with the rubbernecking Hawk. John Wilson of HBO's *How To With John Wilson* subsequently interviewed the car's owner about the moment, with Wilson telling the owner that his car burning to a crisp (thanks to a rat's nest in the engine) was worth it in the end because he got to meet Tony Hawk. It's moments like these where it's clear that Hawk can no longer escape his own fame, even with its most trivial moments compounding themselves. His fame has even transcended generations, with Riley Hawk, Tony's son, making news for dating Frances Bean Cobain, the daughter of '90s icons Kurt Cobain and Courtney Love. One could imagine that would be a tiring existence, living with the knowledge that everything you do is deemed fit for public consumption and criticism. But Hawk has generally excelled at self-awareness. When rapper Lil Nas X pointed out that the backlash he received for his allegedly a scene from *New Jack City*, where his character is crying as he's about to shoot his best friend played by Allen Payne, along with the caption "when the race war is happening and I gotta kill tony hawk." Hawk's response of "I appreciate the hesitation though" went viral and became a meme in itself.

Not many celebrities would dare to or succeed at playing in the murky waters of online memedom like Hawk has, but his wit and the sturdy shield of treasured public persona carry him through. Hawk's noteriety and influence are not just a testament to his skill as an athlete (the reason why people first started to pay attention) but also to his uncanny ability to self-promote. In March 2022, a trailer was released for *Tony Hawk: Until the Wheels Fall Off*, an HBO documentary produced by the Duplass Brothers and directed by Sam Jones. The film traces Hawk's life from early childhood to skateboard prodigy and then superstar, ultimately asking how long the 53-year-old legend can continue to skate at such a high level. The day the trailer dropped, Hawk broke his femur skateboarding — a wheel had, at least temporarily, fallen off. Hawk soon began to give updates on his recovery status on social media. He would present an award at the Oscars just weeks later, walking the red carpet with a cane. Then, just over a month after snapping the largest bone in his body while in his early 50s, Hawk posted an Instagram video of himself cautiously pumping up and down the smaller ramps in his indoor skatepark. His millions of followers witnessed his recovery, and the comment sections on these posts were full of encouraging messages like "Do it for you. You always have. You have

Eventually, the key ingredient to Hawk's success and longevity became clear. Whether it's hawking Subway or inviting the world to watch his recovery from a devastating injury, Hawk knows how to draw an audience and remain a continually relevant cultural force. His skills as a marketer are built on the same foundation that made him an iconic skateboarder: an unparalleled ability to spin.

10

Buttons Pushed

The doom spiral of the later entries in the *Pro Skater* series was a result of creative stagnation and rushing the product, of the producers and the publishers of the games being beholden to release deadlines and not having the opportunity to ensure that what they were putting out was something that people actually wanted to play, not just an increasingly poor imitation of itself. "I think it was one of those things where you have that audience, you know they want more, and you just don't give them something that's worthy. And then all the suits decide, 'Well clearly people don't want skateboarding games anymore.' Well, yes, they do. They just want a better one," Chris Rausch, who worked on the first six titles in the *Pro Skater* franchise, said of the fan fallout after *Pro Skater 5*. As hard as it is to make a consistently good thing, it's even harder to make it quickly.

Progress, when rushed and not given the space or help to mature, leads to mistakes, backsteps, and tense board meetings with executives sheepishly flipping through PowerPoint slides as sales figures slide further down the screen. But *Pro Skater*'s self-immolation doesn't mean all was for naught, or that it didn't have an impact on the lives of millions. *Pro Skater* defined an entire genre of video games and inspired countless people to skate, people who had never considered that skateboarding could be for them. Pro skateboarder Keith Denley told *Al's Skate House* newsletter that he "started skating shortly after getting hooked on the first Tony Hawk video game, and I grew up in an almost entirely white suburb. Seeing [Kareem Campbell] in the roster of characters was inspiring cause it was confirmation that other black skaters actually existed." Jordyn Barratt, an Olympic skateboarder for Team USA, had not even existed on this planet for an entire year when *Pro Skater* was released but still recognizes the impact, sharing in *Pretending I'm a Superman*, "I think having Elissa Steamer in the video game was a huge step forward for women's skateboarding, just because it showed inclusion and . . . girls who did play the game and wanted to skate as a girl, they got to be able to skate as Elissa, and I think that's super rad and like I'm thankful for the people who created the game to have done that . . . I'm sure it opened a lot of girls' eyes."

That's real influence and impact. No abysmally selling, shoddy skateboard-shaped controller — a weak peripheral rip-off of the *Guitar Hero* trend — can take that away from *Pro Skater*. That's not to say the game and its many iterations were beacons of progressivism and inclusion; in fact, some parts of them haven't aged well at all. From a bizarre series-wide in-joke where you might stumble across a human character staring amorously at the backside of a goat,[15] to a challenge in the Venice Beach level of *Pro Skater 2* called "Ollie the Magic Bum," where you ollie over a homeless person to complete it.

Juvenile and cruel. Impactful and inspiring. That's a lot of clashing nuance to pack into a video game. And for many years, for better or worse, *Pro Skater* was the popular mainstream's window into skateboarding culture, a piece of interactive media that gave you glimpses of what the world it was based on might be like. Enough to get the point across, enough to get you intrigued. Are the games an accurate reflection of skateboarding? No. Not really. They're arcade-like, occasionally cartoonish, and, as Jamie Thomas once worried, definitely cheesy. But they're fun and had the desired effect: they got people interested in this wheeled wooden toy.

Suppose the *Pro Skater* franchise hadn't reached the heights it has, helping to legitimize the act of skateboarding in the eyes of the everyday person and proving that there is a substantial audience for skateboarding content in all its forms. In that case, it's a real possibility that the more accurate and nuanced representations of skateboarding in media wouldn't have been given their subsequent chances. Like HBO's *Betty*, a fictional comedy series that follows a diverse group of young

---

15 In the Hollywood level of *American Wasteland*, if you happen to break through a nondescript portion of wall several stories in the air that you can only reach via a series of convoluted grinds, you'll stumble across a construction worker in a hotel room cheering as they inspect a goat's rear end, the animal itself standing on a bed.

female skaters as they maneuver their ways through life in New York City; or Bing Liu's 2018 Oscar-nominated documentary, *Minding the Gap*, which tells the story of Liu and his friends' complicated upbringings in their Rust Belt hometown, revealing the cracks in their lives and how love seeps in and out of them.

These are stories told not just about skateboarding but about skateboarders. Highlighting the joyous and heartrending experiences that define them, and all of us broadly, as people. That wooden toy with wheels is just the mortar that holds their stories together. These are representations that move beyond the hackneyed narratives of rival skate gangs featured in films like *Thrashin'*, which, while a mostly fun '80s romp, didn't reflect the life that regular skateboarders lived. It wasn't until a critical mass of skateboarders existed that more authentic stories about skateboarding would get told, because that's when it would become commercially viable for studios to greenlight them for the now reliably large audience. There's something of a formula to this. A recent and similar parallel: "nerd" culture. Initially, nerds — those seen as socially awkward and believed to be flush with intellect but lacking in athletic ability and popularity — were bullied for reading comic books and hosting Dungeons & Dragons campaigns in their basements, but then there was a shift. *The Big Bang Theory*, featuring a cast of self-identified nerd characters, became one of the most popular sitcoms of the 2010s and the Marvel Cinematic Universe, part of the urtext of nerd interests, started to put pop culture in a tight full nelson with its big green Hulk hands. While it can certainly feel predatory when these industries start to pull from cultures they finally find bankable, it doesn't mean there can't be positive results.

Projects like *Betty* and *Minding the Gap* focus on the lives of Black, Asian, Latinx, and LGBTQ+ skateboarders who historically haven't had the opportunity to publicly tell their stories. While it's a bit of a nebulous task to link *Pro Skater* to leading a shift from skateboarding's predominantly straight, white male demographic toward a more inclusive one, it undoubtedly succeeded in bringing skateboarding into countless new homes. And while a lot of representative weight rested on the shoulders of Elissa Steamer and Kareem Campbell's characters, this video game is still often cited as an animating moment for women and skateboarders of color, including *Minding the Gap*'s Keire Johnson.

"I had these two friends growing up, they were brothers. I went over there one day after school and we started playing *Tony Hawk's Pro Skater 2* and I saw that there was a Black skateboarder, and I was like, 'Oh my god, this is kinda cool.' I feel like if I didn't see Kareem Campbell in that, though, I probably wouldn't have been interested. But because I saw [that] representation, I felt like it was something that I could do. I was expected to play football and basketball and stuff like that. I was like, you know, I'm probably just going to skate," Johnson would say in *Pretending I'm a Superman*.

If it's hard to calculate the cause of a demographic shift, it's even harder to hurry social progress. Skateboarding has done a lot of growing and changing over the past two decades, not all of it quick or complete. But it's happening, however slowly. Queer-centric skate crews and companies like Unity, There, and Glue are doing some of the coolest work in the industry today. froSkate is a Black- and queer-led collective that "provide[s] inclusive experiences, resources and equity for the BIPOC, non-traditional skateboarding community" in the Chicago area. Nations Skate Youth is an Indigenous-led organization that travels to communities across Canada to provide workshops that "[empower] Indigenous youth to embrace their right to self-determination through the positive impact of skateboarding."

Companies, collectives, and organizations geared toward casting skateboarding's net even wider have been popping up all over the world in recent years. SkatePal is "a non-profit organisation supporting communities throughout Palestine, promoting the social, health and wellbeing benefits of skateboarding to enhance the lives of local youth." In Addis Ababa, Ethiopia Skate has worked to build the first free-to-use skateparks in the country and foster a young community of skateboarders. These initiatives are emblematic of the grassroots DIY ethos that skateboarding was built on, starting in earnest with rickety wooden vert ramps hammered into place in backyards and the swimming pools drained by teenaged skateboarders and their friends to ride in. When an insular skateboarding industry propped up mainly straight, white, cisgender male skateboarders, social media would help level the playing field. In our online world, anyone can release content and build an audience, which helps to feed inspiration to new skaters who don't see themselves adequately represented in mainstream skate culture. It was in this precise way that groups like Unity and froSkate were able to build community so quickly via Instagram. *Pro Skater* had much the same effect — and philosophy — in the late '90s. It showed that skateboarding is a thing *everyone* can do.

In June 2020, after a nearly five-year hiatus following the disastrous fallout of *Tony Hawk's Pro Skater 5*, Activision released a new Hawk-branded skateboarding video game. Sort of. *Tony Hawk's Pro Skater 1 + 2* is a remaster of the series' most beloved installments, a smart play at the general public's constantly stimulated nostalgia centers. Because despite the disappointing last efforts of the *Pro Skater* series, its fans have held on to their good early memories. It also doesn't hurt that Tony Hawk is as savvy and relevant a marketeer as ever. And really, when you break down the essence of the first games, they are simply fun, no matter what decade you happen to be playing them in.

To Activision and developer Vicarious Visions' credit, they were faithful to that original formula and stuck the landing. *IGN* gave *Pro Skater 1+2* a 9/10, saying, "It turns out going backwards has been the best step forward Activision has taken with the Tony Hawk series in nearly 15 years." The game became the fastest-selling entry in the franchise's history, easily eclipsing a million copies sold in just ten days. It was eventually awarded Best Sports/Racing Game at the

Game Awards in 2020. That's an unquestionably triumphant return to form. But while the remaster of the game stuck to the original two entries' scripts, there were also new elements. Like the impressive graphics that only contemporary gaming consoles offer and stat-building that's transferable across the two games. These are all advancements that came with time, gradual progress, and new technological capabilities. Then there are the changes that happened outside of the video game world that came to be reflected inside of it.

Close to half of *Pro Skater 1+2*'s character roster are women, non-binary, and people of color. It's easily the series' most diverse cast to date. The game's influence on the outside world inspired the people now in the game itself, as Leo Baker would tell *Hypebeast* about his inclusion in the game. "Because I was able to see Elissa in the game, there was a part of me that was like, 'Oh, I can be a pro skater.' Now, there's even more representation. I think that's really beautiful. As a queer skateboarder, I feel like it's a real win for queers who skate, that there's trans representation in this video game that's extremely influential."

The game's create-a-character function enables players to make an avatar of any skin tone, size, and none of the body types are gendered — small changes that go a long way when it comes to being able to see one's self on the screen. And while there's still room to grow (the "Ollie the Magic Bum" challenge in the Venice Beach level made it into the remake, even with two decades' worth of hindsight), this maturation process seems to be done in earnest. Before *Pro Skater 1 + 2*'s release, Hawk announced that they'd be changing the name of a trick in the game known as a "mute" grab to a "Weddle" grab to honor the trick's creator Chris Weddle properly.

Weddle, who is deaf, invented the trick in the early '8os, and skaters at the time, not being the most perceptive or sensitive bunch, misnamed it in a particularly ableist fashion. "I am deaf, not mute," Weddle told Hawk in a conversation in advance of the game's release, prompting Hawk and the developers to take action, with the Birdman explaining the decision in an Instagram post: "So as we embark on the upcoming @tonyhawkthegame demo release, some of you might notice a trick name change: The Weddle Grab. It's going to be challenging to break the habit of saying the old name but I think Chris deserves the recognition." Slow, steady progress, but progress nonetheless.

Hawk, Neversoft, and Activision made a video game about a culture that rejected the mainstream spotlight and was wary of outsiders. The game was an unprecedented hit, and those outsiders who first became acquainted with skateboarding by mashing buttons suddenly wanted in. Soon, skateboarding's ranks grew — this decades-spanning series an integral part of the growth of the skateboarding industry itself. But the legacy of *Tony Hawk's Pro Skater* shouldn't just be measured in dollar signs. We should also consider its personal impact on the untold numbers of people it inspired to spend their lives trying to be good at, failing, sometimes succeeding, but ultimately loving riding a skateboard. That this video game contributed to changing a culture so dramatically that the inclusivity it inadvertently inspired would eventually circle back to changing the game itself.

And if your only memory of *Pro Skater* is a vague wash of crashing around the Warehouse as two minutes of Goldfinger's "Superman" played on loop, the leftover Stuffed Crust pizza you nuked as an after-school snack still steaming on the plate beside you, that's alright too. It is just a video game, after all. But maybe, once your older sibling was mercifully done playing, you finally got a grip on the controller and entered an entirely new world — one where you could do things you couldn't dream of before. Perhaps that's when you got a big, life-changing idea: *Hey, I should go outside and try that.*

Sources

2021 Essential Facts about the Video Game Industry. Entertainment Software Association, 2021.

"720°: Arcade Video Game Published 36 Years Ago by Atari Games." *Gaming History*. https://www.arcade-history.com/?n=720_degrees&page=detail&id=23.

Agnello, Anthony John. "Tricks, Kickflips, and Thumbsticks: An Oral History of the Making of *Tony Hawk's Pro Skater*." *The Ringer*, August 30, 2019.

"Apocalypse." *Next Generation*, January 1997.

Barrow, Ted. "Skateboarding Is Not Art." *Jenkem*, January 7, 2019.

The Berrics. "Tony Hawk Interviews the Original *THPS* Cast," YouTube, May 15, 2020. https://youtu.be/L1R1Ch-2JBs?t=104.

"The Best-Selling Games of 2000," *ZD Net*, January 11, 2001.

Borden, Iain. *Skateboarding and the City: A Complete History*. London: Bloomsbury Visual Arts, 2019.

Brown, Al. "Honoring the Lineage of Black Skateboarders with Black Skateboarders." *Al's Skate House*, February 12, 2022.

Carter, Thom James. "What Gaming Does to Your Brain — and How You Might Benefit." *Wired*, June 26, 2021.

Childers, Chad. "Goldfinger's John Feldman: 'Tony Hawk's Pro Skater' Impact Was Greater Than Anyone Could Have Imagined." *Loudwire*, June 16, 2020.

Cohen, Matt. "13 Quotes: Highlights from Ian MacKaye's Library of Congress Lecture." *SPIN*, May 8, 2013.

Cook, Forrest. "Skateboarding Legend Kareem Campbell Has Plenty to Say on His New Podcast." *Dallas Observer*, January 26, 2021.

Cork, Jeff. "How Takafumi Fujisawa Created the Original PlayStation's Startup Sound." *PlayStation Blog*, December 5, 2019.

The Escapist. "*Tony Hawk's Pro Skater*, Pizza Hut, and the Greatest Video Game Demo Ever." YouTube, October 22, 2022. http://www.youtube.com/watch?v=J72RbojfpG4.

Fielder, Lauren. "Female Skater Joins Tony Hawk." *Gamespot*, April 27, 2000.

froSkate. https://www.froskate.com/.

Game Brain. "Talking to the Original Designer of *Tony Hawk's Pro Skater*." YouTube, January 1, 2018.

Gerstmann, Jeff. "*Tony Hawk's American Wasteland Review*." *Gamespot*, March 30, 2006.

Ginner, Garrett. "Street Skating in LA With Friends!" YouTube, February 18, 2022.

Gunsmith, Skaidris. "The Story Behind the Aussie Band That Just Plays *Tony Hawk Pro Skater* Covers." *Kotaku*, July 5, 2019.

Gür, Ludvig, dir. *Pretending I'm a Superman: The Tony Hawk Video Game Story*. Wood Entertainment, 2020.

Hart, Torrey. "Skateboarding Veterans Rune Glifber, Dallas Oberholzer Compete in Tokyo." *NBC Olympics*, August 4, 2021.

Hauser, Henry , Janine Schaults, Kristofer Lenz, Matt Melis, and Michael Madden. "Ranking: Every Bob Dylan Album from Worst to Best." *Consequence of Sound*, March 31, 2017.

Horror_spooky. "Skate or Die — Review." *GameFAQs*, January 20, 2015. https://gamefaqs.gamespot.com/nes/587621-skate-or-die/reviews/159871.

"How Many Skateboarders Are There in the World?" *Surfer Today*, August, 20, 2021.

"International Association of Skateboard Companies." Boardriding.com. https://www.boardriding.com/associations/international-association-of-skateboard-companies-iasc.

Kennedy, Sam. "Sony's Demo Pizza Party." *Gamespot*, April 27, 2000.

"Kevin Kowalski Interview," *Bones*, https://bones.com/vip-kevin-kowalski.

Klein, Lucas. "Skateboard Games — A History of Skateboarding Video Games." Everskate. https://everskate.com/skateboard-games.html.

Leak, Brian. "'Tony Hawk's Pro Skater,' Hugely Influential in Both Music + Video Games, Turns 20." *Loudwire*, August 30, 2019.

Lin, Brittney. "Diversity in Gaming Report: An Analysis of Diversity in Video Game Characters." *DiamondLobby*, May 14, 2022.

Lipscombe, Daniel. "How a Troubled Game Starring Bruce Willis Led to the Skateboarding Revolution." *Eurogamer*, June 17, 2018.

Longbottom, John. "An Oral History of the *Tony Hawk's Pro Skater* Soundtrack, by Tony Hawk and John Feldman." *Kerrang!*, January 4, 2022.

Lynch, Teresa, Jessica E. Tompkins, Irene I. van Driel, and Niki Fritz. "Sexy, Strong, and Secondary: A Content Analysis of Female Characters in Video Games Across 31 Years." *Journal of Communication*, August 2016.

Mac, James. "Birdman: Or the Unexpected Virtue of a *Tony Hawk Pro Skater* Cover Band." *Forte*, April 2020.

Malley, Clare. "For Leo Baker, Joining *Tony Hawk's Pro Skater 1 + 2* Is a Dream Come True." *Hypebeast*, September 3, 2020.

"Market and Industry Information." *Transworld Skatebaording*, November 8, 2001.

Martin, Matt. "*Tony Hawk: Shred* Flops with Only 3000 Units Sold in US." *Games Industry. biz*, November 17, 2010.

Michna, Ian. "The Andrew Reynolds Interview." *Jenkem*, September 2, 2014.

Muhammad, Amir. "Game Cred: Y'all Skate Too? Examining *Tony Hawk's Pro Skater*'s Curious Representation." *Film Cred*, October 1, 2021.

Nations Skate Youth. https://nationsskateyouth.com/.

"Number of Skateboarding Participants in the United States from 2010 to 2021." Statista Research Department, 2022.

Oddheader. "Solving Tony Hawk Game Mysteries with Series Producer." YouTube, August 16, 2020. https://youtu.be/yqOQGNqGq_c?t=322.

Ombler, Mat. "'It inspired a generation': Tony Hawk on How the Pro Skater Video Games Changed Lives." *The Guardian*, September 4, 2019.

Parkin, Simon. "*Tony Hawk's Pro Skater 5* Review." *Eurogamer*, October 2, 2015.

Perry, Doug. "*Thrasher: Skate and Destroy*." *IGN*, December 6, 1999.

Perry, Douglass C. "*Tony Hawk's Underground 2*." *IGN*, December 12, 2018.

Pickert, Katie. "A Brief History of the X Games." *Time*, January 22, 2009.

Pullan, Brandon. "Throwback Thursday: Priest Who Set Speed Climbing Record." *Gripped Indoor Climbing*, October 4, 2018.

"RDN and Community Celebrate New Skatepark on Gabriola Island." *Municipal World*, May 30, 2022.

ReclaimedVHS. "RAD — X-Games Vert Best Trick 1999." YouTube, December 25, 2009. https://www.youtube.com/watch?v=rM6t5_sLPfk&ab_channel =ReclaimedVHS.

Reilly, Luke. *Tony Hawk's Pro Skater 1+2 Remake Review.* *IGN*, February 25, 2021.

RIDE Channel. "*Animal Chin* 30 Years — Recreating the Invert Photo ¾." YouTube, October 30, 2016. https://www.youtube.com/watch?v=2_CAFTP4B9Q.

RIDE Channel. "Tony Hawk Lands 900 at 48!" YouTube, June 27, 2016.

Schwartz, Drew. "Tony Hawk Took a Selfie with This Guy after His Car Burst into Flames." *Vice*, May 3, 2017.

Schwinghammer, Stefan. "Elissa Steamer — Just Skateboarding." *SOLO*, November 2, 2018.

Scotti, Lawrence. "Tony Hawk Faces Backlash after Launching New NFT Project." *Dexerto*, February 5, 2022.

Silent (@silenthooper). "When the race war . . ." Twitter, October 20, 2018.

Silva, Marty. *Tony Hawk's Pro Skater*, Pizza Hut, and the Greatest Video Game Demo Ever." *The Escapist*, April 14, 2020.

"Skate Boardin' — Absolute Entertainment — Atari 2600." *AtariAge*, https://atariage.com /manual_html_page.php?SoftwareLabelID=432.

"Skateboard Market Size, Share & Trends Analysis Report by Product, By End User, By Region, And Segment Forecasts, 2019–2025." Grand View Research, 2015.

The Skatepark Project. https://skatepark.org/.

Smith, Jonathan. "Maybe We Shouldn't Be So Quick to Idolize a Gay-Bashing Skateboarder." *Vice*, August 19, 2014.

Stanley, Jack. "Geoff Rowley Is Still Stoked on Skating." *Hypebeast*, June 29,2021.

Statistics Canada. "2001 Community Profiles." *2001 Census*. Ottawa: Statistics Canada, 2001. https://www12.statcan.gc.ca/English/profil01/CP01/Details/Page.cfm?

"Street Sk8ter," *Next Generation*, June 1999.

Tach, Dave. "How Arcane Kids Replaced Tony Hawk's 900 with a Time Wizard in Perfect Stride." *Polygon*, June 22, 2013.

Tony Hawk. https://tonyhawk.com.

Tony Hawk (@tonyhawk). "Did this trick once . . ." Twitter, March 23, 2021.

Tony Hawk (@tonyhawk). "For nearly 40 years . . . ." Instagram, August 12, 2020.

"*Tony Hawk's Pro Skater*." Metacritic, August 31, 1999.

"*Tony Hawk's Pro Skater 2*." *IGN*, December, 12, 2018.

"*Tony Hawk's Pro Skater 2*." Metacritic, September 20, 2000.

Tony Hawk's Pro Skater 1 and 2. "Chad Muska: Behind the Scenes Tony Hawk's Pro Skater 1 and 2." YouTube. https://youtu.be/Pg5O1a5rBFU?t=19.

u/Pieassassin24. "Remember getting PlayStation demos from Pizza Hut." Reddit. March 7, 2019. https://www.reddit.com/r/gaming/comments/aydr3p/remember_getting_playstation _demos_from_pizza_hut/.

Webster, Andrews. "How *Tony Hawk's Pro Skater* Changed the Lives of Some of the World's Biggest Skaters." *The Verge*, July 29, 2020.

Wojnar, Zak. "Steve Caballero, Geoff Rowley, and Andrew Reynolds Interview: *Tony Hawk's Pro Skater 1 & 2*." *ScreenRant*, August 12, 2020.

X Games. "Tony Hawk lands world's first 900 on a skateboard at X Games — 20th year anniversary," YouTube, June 27, 2019. https://youtu.be/ItI4UWoTPCI?t=180.

ZexyZek. "*Epic Skate 3 Glitches*." YouTube, July 20, 2017.

Images

Screen capture from *Skate Boardin'* (Absolute Entertainment, 1987).

Screen capture from *California Games* (Epyx, 1987).

Photo of Lance Mountain, Steve Caballero, Mike McGill, and Tony Hawk by J. Grant Brittain (1987).

Domino meme by originator Stephen Morris, used with permission.

All efforts have been made to contact the owners of quoted materials in this book. If you are the rightful owner, please reach out so that we can address any concerns.

Cole Nowicki is a Vancouver-based writer and lifelong skateboarder. He was a columnist for *King Skateboard Magazine*, lead writer for the acclaimed skateboarding documentary series *Post Radical*, and writes *Simple Magic*, a weekly newsletter about skateboarding, the internet, and other means of escape. His freelance work has appeared in *The Walrus*, *Vice*, *Maisonneuve*, and more.

Acknowledgments

Thank you to Jen, Anita, and everyone at ECW for believing in this book and for the sharp edits and invaluable guidance along the way. It was a true pleasure working on this with y'all.

James, even though as adults we mostly want to beat each other up, I'll always be thankful that you introduced me to skateboarding and pointed my life in the best direction I could have ever imagined it going. I love you and look forward to whooping your ass at Xmas.